DISPENSATIONALISM

Understanding the Basics

J. MICHAEL LESTER

Dispensationalism: Understanding the Basics
Second Edition

Lancaster, CA
JMichaelLester@gmail.com

Scripture quotations taken from *The Holy Bible: King James Version*, public domain.

Dedication

No book is truly the work of just one person. There are always teammates that stand behind a writer, encouraging, supporting, and cheering all the way.

I know I'll not be able to name everyone and any omissions aren't meant as a slight. I sincerely appreciate all who have helped bring this project to print.

First, I'm grateful for my wife, Jen. She encourages me to write and knows that I greatly enjoy it. With over twenty-five years of marriage and ministry, she truly is God's gift to me. Her questions, comments, and feedback always help me push to continually try to reach my audience – true beginners.

Secondly, for those first readers who provided valuable insight – from new Christians, from theologians, from faithful church members. Each perspective allowed me to refine the contents to hit my target audience – the "dispensational newbie!"

I would also like to thank colleagues who challenge me to think, who test my assertions, all with an iron-sharpening-iron relationship. These co-laborers have strengthened this project.

I'd like to also dedicate this to those who invested in me early. You saw something and believed in me. To my parents, thank you for your investment into me. To my grandparents, now in Heaven, all of those commentaries you purchased for me have left its mark. To my Aunt Tobie, you introduced me to dispensational thinking with Clarence Larkin's writings. I'm forever grateful.

Finally, I dedicate this book to all past and future students who have sat or will sit in my *Introduction to Dispensationalism* class.

Many of the questions you have asked through the years have found their way here to help the next generation. Thank you.

For those friends who are the unnamed and unsung heroes, you are not unforgotten. I just couldn't let the dedication become longer than the book! While each of these have helped strengthen what is written, for what remains I, and I alone, am responsible.

Contents

CHAPTER TWO

CHAPTER THREE

CHAPTER FOUR

CHAPTER FIVE

CHAPTER SIX

CHAPTER SEVEN

Foreword

Let's start by allowing me to say, "Hello!" Thanks for picking up a copy of this book. I really hope it's a help. Writers like to write about the truths they are most passionate about, and this book is no exception to that principle.

Dispensationalism is something that has become a passion for me gradually – a passion that wasn't birthed overnight. Yet, now I enjoy talking about it, teaching it, and yes – even writing about it! This is true even when people have no idea what I'm talking about. So, whether you are a card-carrying dispensationalist, someone who isn't sure, or just want to know how "the other side" thinks – I'm glad we can have this conversation.

I guess the reason that this is such a passion is because it is so closely connected to the way I understand the Bible. To me, one of the most important things in life is to understand what God says to us. Dispensationalism is a key to understanding His Word in its context. Throughout this book, I plan to make my case for this!

So, who am I? I grew up in a pastor's home. I accepted Christ as my Savior when I was eleven years old. Later, when I was in high school, I surrendered to preach. I can still remember going forward on a Sunday night, praying with my dad, and then announcing in front of our country church, "God wants me to be a preacher." Little did I know how much that one decision in March of 1989 would change my life's direction.

Upon announcing that decision, my parents and grandparents bought me all of Oliver B. Greene's collection. After all, books were the tools of preachers (long before the age of digital books and Bible software!). My aunt, along with other family members bought me all of Clarence Larkin's books. My theological training - even before Bible college or seminary - was rooted in dispensational theology (even if I didn't know it at the time!).

Around 1992-1993, someone gave me Charles Ryrie's book on dispensationalism. My first experience with it didn't go so well. Hated it! I didn't understand the culture, the terms, the big picture. I didn't finish it. (Don't worry, eventually I developed a great respect for that book and have read it through on numerous occasions now!)

As newlyweds in 1995, my wife and I moved to Lancaster, California to serve in a new Bible college – West Coast Baptist College. Several years later, I would have the opportunity to teach my first *Introduction to Dispensationalism* course in a Bible college setting. It quickly became my favorite class (I can't say it was the students' favorite!). I teach it every semester on-campus and I teach it a few times each year online as well.

Time passes, and yet that first day of class still remains the same. Students walk into the first day with that same look... the look that communicates "I'm overwhelmed, I'm scared, and by the way – what is dispensationalism!" I listen to them talk amongst themselves, "What do you know about this class? What's the work load? What is dispensation, anyway? Why is this a required class?" I'm excited on the last day of class when many communicate to me, "I think I'm getting it now!"

Charles Ryrie's book *Dispensationalism* still remains both a classic and the standard. Yet, some have felt that his book presumes some basic knowledge about the subject. Over the years, I have teased about writing a *Dispensationalism for Dummies* guide. This book represents that idea on a more serious, and yet, practical level.

I have no desire or visions of grandeur that this book would ever replace Ryrie's book. I confess at the very beginning that I am heavily indebted to his work. My goal is much more modest – to

11

simply prepare a generation of Christian leaders to be able to appreciate Ryrie's classic.

The subject of dispensationalism has great bearing on one's hermeneutics (a term that deals with how we interpret the Bible). It is not a novelty to be quickly dismissed. Nor is it a subject that one merely "studies for a grade." The principles of dispensationalism along with its three non-negotiables provide a road map into understanding God's past dealings with Israel, His present plan with the church, and the future of a coming literal kingdom in which Christ sits upon the throne of David.

It is my hope that future generations of Bible preachers and teachers will understand the need for a normal, historical-grammatical hermeneutic to finding the single meaning of the God-inspired text that has been left for us.

And so, I invite you to enter a conversation with me as we learn about the basics of dispensationalism. This book is informal, it's casual by design. This isn't a book written to the academy; rather, it's written for those in the church seats who would like to understand this topic without being intimidated by what they don't know already.

J. Michael Lester
Academic Dean, West Coast Baptist College
August 2020

Introduction

LET'S START WITH WHY

"Once you learn to read, you will be forever free."
Frederick Douglass

Why another book? Even more importantly, does anyone even *care* about reading another book on dispensationalism?! Just the mere mention of this system and you find quickly that it is either accepted by the masses or demonized as coming out of the pit of hell! Rarely is there an in-between position!

I'm fervent about this topic – it's the subject of one of my favorite classes I teach at West Coast Baptist College.[1] But I get it – not everyone shares my passion. Some of my own students, on that first day, aren't so passionate. At times, my own kids haven't shared my enthusiasm – and being young is not an acceptable excuse.

However, the students that I teach do have a love for God, a commitment to truth, and a strong love for the Word of God. When they come into class, their confidence is shaken. They aren't quite sure what they've gotten into; they are worried about the work

---

[1] I have worked at this school since 1995 when it started. It is a ministry-training school with a single focus: Training Labors for the Harvest. Want to know more? http://wcbc.edu

load, and they don't really know if they can believe the good things the upper classmen are telling them!

A great joy for me is to have these students fourteen or fifteen weeks later say things like, "I am a dispensationalist!" More than a few have said, "This was my favorite class…" – which doesn't really mean a whole lot – but I still enjoy hearing it! This book is my attempt to invigorate my love for this topic into believers outside the four walls of my classroom. In short, I want you to become so excited to learn about dispensationalism, that this book leaves you wanting more!

As I've talked with people over the years, I find a common thread. Many grew up under dispensational preaching, but never heard the term. They may have carried a Scofield Bible; they may have been taught pre-tribulationalism; they may have heard it often stated that New Testament believers are not under the law. They may have read the *Left Behind* series! They may have heard their pastor say something about following the common sense of the text or "The Bible cannot mean what it never meant." Yep, they may have had a lot of exposure to dispensationalism without even knowing it.

Steve Gregg, a non-dispensationalist, recognizes that dispensationalism "has become the official theology of some of America's largest denominations."[2] It is the *de facto* theological system for many – whether they know it or not. Not only should we have exposure to dispensationalism, I believe we should embrace it and defend it.

Perhaps you're like those students who enter my class and wonder, "What in the world is dispensationalism?!" It may be that our twenty-first century churches *describe* dispensationalism without

---

[2] Steve Gregg, "Is Dispensationalism Indispensable," Feb 7, 2015. https://www.equip.org/article/dispensationalism-indispensable/.

defining it. It's part of the sub-culture, just out of sight but always present. Then one day, the "Aha!" moment comes when the pieces fall together and you realize, "I've been taught dispensationalism all along."

My hope is that once you finish this book, two things will happen. First, you will know what dispensationalism is. Second, you will claim it as your approach to understanding God's Word. In short, I'm hoping your "Aha!" moment comes sooner than later.

As children, we were not *educated* per se – we were *indoctrinated!* And, by the way, I'm not saying that's bad. Our parents had a responsibility to do their best to shape a worldview, value system, and biblical understanding in a relatively short time. If you are a parent, then perhaps you can identify when you bring your newborn home. At that moment, you think you have forever to train them. However, after over twenty-five years of marriage, I understand the phrase, "Time goes by so fast." Two of our children are married, one has a child, and my wife and I are grandparents!

Many preachers joke that they were "drug babies." In fact, I recently heard Dr. David Jeremiah make the exact statement as well.[3] The statement means something like, "I was *drug* to church Sunday mornings, nights, and midweek prayer services. In essence, it's a tacit admission that we have been indoctrinated – that we have had biblical truth instilled in us. Many of us share Timothy's testimony, "And that from a child, thou hast known the holy Scriptures…"

All of that indoctrination is tested as you head off to college and seminary. There, you begin to realize that some people are against your views – or, they've never even heard that view. In this context, dispensationalism really is no different. It has its friends; it

---

[3] The sermon, "Living with Confidence in a Chaotic World," can be found here: https://www.youtube.com/watch?v=-jz4DEljlVw.

has its critics. Frankly, it can't be the dispensationalism of your parents…each of us must own it personally and explain it clearly.

My journey

I grew up in smaller, country churches in Georgia. In our churches, everyone knew everyone. Often, we were related to many in the church or as close to being relatives as possible. We attended revivals and camp meetings. We believed in supporting missionaries. We loved God and country. We quoted the Bible and Scofield. 'Nuff said!

My dad was my pastor. (By default, this meant I was a reoccurring star in sermon illustrations!) My dad surrendered to preach after coming home from Vietnam and right before I was born. He started pastoring his first church around the time I was ten or eleven. I can't remember a time when I wasn't in church.

Contemplate what I am saying…we were *always* in church. It's just what we did. My granddad on my mom's side was a pastor. My great-granddad on my dad's side was a preacher. Many of my uncles are preachers. No one was shocked when I was sixteen years old and announced that God had called me to preach. Some would have been shocked if I didn't!

Growing up in a pastor's home means that you get to live in a glass house. For some church members, your parents are too strict and for others they're not strict enough. Yet, this type of scrutiny never really affected our family. My parents – really, my extended family – were kind, gracious, and giving people.

As soon as I let my spiritual direction be known – that I was going to be a preacher – family rallied behind me and encouraged me. One uncle bought me a Strong's concordance with my name engraved (this was before there was Logos Bible software or any of its competitors).

I mentioned previously that my grandparents and parents purchased a large preacher's commentary set for me from Oliver B. Greene. It was my aunt who purchased for me some books that really introduced me to dispensational thinking. I was sixteen or seventeen and reading Clarence Larkin's *Spirit World*, his *Book of Daniel* or *Revelation* – and, of course, I had the big book of dispensational truths and charts. I was fascinated.

I also began to take the time to read Scofield's notes in his study Bible. Granted, I didn't have much discernment then and his words were probably on the same level of authority as Paul. I mean, after all, his words *were in the Bible*. I quickly learned that Scofield wasn't inspired, but, still, I was being handed tools that would affect the way I would read the Bible over thirty years later.

I'm not sure when I learned that dispensationalism was a system of theology. I'm not sure when I realized that not every believer read the Bible the same way as I did. I can remember a few things, though. I can remember a guest preacher claiming to be a spiritual Jew. I was only a teen, but that didn't sound right to me. I can remember another friend reading a verse about "binding the strong man," and use that as justification for not serving God. Again, I was only a teen, but I knew that meaning couldn't be found in the text.

I didn't know it at the time, but my passion for a normal, historical-grammatical interpretation was already being developed. My belief that the church is separate from Israel was already being developed. Oh, yeah - there's one more thing I remember - being assigned to read Charles Ryrie's book in college. I didn't mind reading...but I wanted to read books of my own choosing. An assigned book felt like drudgery to me and frankly, Ryrie's classic fell on deaf ears the first time.

After college and now serving in a ministry position, I was provided a lot of exposure to good books, good preachers, and colleagues that could mentor me. When I chose to read Ryrie on my own, it was a totally different experience. All the pieces came together for me and I begin to say, "I'm a dispensationalist."

One day at the Bible college I serve in, our Bible faculty were meeting with the department chair. We began to discuss the topic of dispensationalism. We were looking at our curriculum and realized that while students were being indirectly exposed to this type of thinking, there was no one class where students were taught dispensationalism. That was the day I begin to prepare materials for a new course that would soon become my favorite one - Introduction to Dispensationalism.

I still assign my students to read Ryrie, but I'm afraid many of them read it like I did my first time! It's an assignment; they don't quite understand it, they don't like it, etc. I've looked over the years for a pre-Ryrie book – one that would start by assuming the reader knew nothing about dispensationalism and explain to them what it is. While there are some great resources out there, I never found just exactly what I was looking for.

Students can be your biggest critics or your biggest cheerleaders. In this context, students have asked me, "Why don't you write a basic book that could be an introduction to dispensationalism?" I've deferred with, "I've got other projects…" or "I don't have the time," or "Other people are better qualified…" Yet, here we are. In the late spring and early summer of 2020, CoVid-19 gave us all a little more time.

From the curious teen preacher to now an academic dean, my goal is to help others who are taking that same journey. I don't know the reason you're holding this book, but I look forward to talking you through what a dispensationalist is.

There is a difference

I believe one of the reasons I am so passionate is because there really is a difference.[4] It matters how we handle God's Word. How we understand Scripture affects the way we live our lives. For a preacher of the Word, there is a high calling to stand and say, "This is what the text means." We don't want to lead people astray.

A friend sent me Michael Vlach's *You Might be a Dispensationalist if…* list. Vlach had offered a session at a conference with this title. Growing up in Georgia, I'm vaguely familiar with Jeff Foxworthy's *You might be a redneck if…* lines. I can't vouch for what the "punchlines" were, but the title of his routine is indelibly impressed upon my mind. So, Vlach's wordplay on his title definitely captured my attention. Here were his six points. *You might be a dispensationalist if…*

1. You believe the primary meaning of the Old Testament passages are found in the Old Testament.
2. You believe that national Israel is not a type that finds its significance ended with the Church.
3. You reject replacement theology.
4. You believe that Jews and Gentiles can be unified in salvation and that there is a future for the nation of Israel.
5. You believe that the nation of Israel will be saved / restored with a role to the nations after the Second Coming.
6. You believe that believing Gentiles can be the seed of Abraham without becoming spiritual Jews or part of Israel.[5]

---

[4] Renald Showers wrote a book on dispensationalism with that title (*There Really is a Difference*). So, I had to come up with a new title!

[5] Vlach offered this at a Shepherd's Conference in 2010 at Grace Community Church. His session is archived here: https://www.gracechurch.org/(X(1)S(wggtdua3oxepbc0ojqrai25g))/sermon

Vlach's list does a good job of pointing out that differences really exist between dispensational theology and other forms or systems of theology. He does so in a good-natured way and should at least provide some grounds for people to think about the issues. Yet, even in his six points, there are still areas that perhaps a new believer doesn't have the background to understand the context.

No matter your theological position, we all have to admit that there are changes between believers in the New Testament and those who lived under the Mosaic Law. The different theological systems each provide their best attempt at answering these differences. Some are minor (diet) and some are major (the indwelling of the Spirit). Here's a short list of some of the differences between me (and probably you!) and an Old Testament believer:

1. I eat pork, sausage, and bacon...and I love it!
2. I don't eat shellfish - but that has nothing to do with the Mosaic Covenant.
3. I wear clothing that contains mixed fabrics - a definite violation of Leviticus (and no one threatens me with stoning!).
4. I don't bring an animal sacrifice to church with me each week (but wouldn't that get expensive!).
5. I worship on Sundays rather than Saturday.
6. I get counsel from a pastor rather than a priest.
7. I have access to Jesus without going through a priest.
8. I have the permanent indwelling of the Spirit.
9. I'm part of the Bride of Christ (not the wife of Jehovah).

---

s/language/1?page=38&searchministry=shepherdsconference&books=0&c
hapters=0&verses=0.

Differences exist. Both dispensationalists and non-dispensationalists recognize this.[6] I am a dispensationalist for many reasons. However, one reason is that I personally believe dispensationalism does the best job at explaining these differences. I know others disagree with that statement. But, you've given me the opportunity to make a case for dispensationalism by reading this book. I hope you'll see why I believe that.

My promise to you

Before you jump in, let me make a few promises to you. You might figure out as you read this book that I *may* be a little biased! I am a dispensationalist. But, in fairness, I'm not a dispensationalist because I was bred to be one. What you read in the next few chapters is the fruit of personal study – personal study that has only deepened my conviction to reading the Bible as a dispensationalist.

While I have some strong convictions, I promise to present those who disagree with me as charitably as possible. I promise to build a case for why the interpretative method of dispensationalism is the best approach to studying Scripture. I promise to provide sound reasons why God still has a plan for Israel in the future. I promise to help you understand the big picture in God's revelation and the one thing that ties it all together.

I'll do my best to show you that long before a man named John Nelson Darby systematized these teachings, the seeds for them were much earlier. You'll learn how to recognize when dispensations begin and end - what characteristics should you look for.

From a doctrinal perspective, you'll be shown four key doctrinal issues that are affected when a non-dispensational

---

[6] Healthy discussions from those who disagree can take place without someone's personal salvation being revoked or called into question!

approach to the Scriptures is used. Our hermeneutics – the way we interpret the Bible – really do make a difference.

When you finish this book, even if you disagree with my conclusions, you'll at least know what dispensationalism is. You will no longer be able to use a strawman argument against these beliefs (for example, "Dispensationalism teaches more than one way of salvation") in good conscience.

Finally, I promise to keep this "on the bottom shelf" so everyone can take the journey together. Consider this book as my invitation to you for a conversation over coffee. It's casual, it's informative, and it's conversational. Thanks for participating in the conversation!

Chapter 1

DEFINING OUR TERMS

We Cannot Have a Conversation Until We Do

"Most controversies would soon be ended, if those
engaged in them would first accurately define their
terms, and then adhere to their definitions."
Tryon Edwards

Chapter Aims

1. You will understand the importance of defining terms in any conversation.
2. You will have a working definition for *dispensationalism*.
3. You will understand the three non-negotiables that set the parameters for who is a dispensationalist and who is not.
4. You will be able to define auxiliary terms that are often used in this context.

Introduction

When believers hear the phrase, "The beginning of wisdom," they typically connect that to the fear of the Lord. Socrates, a secular philosopher, believed this: "The beginning of wisdom is the definition of terms." I don't fully agree with Socrates – I trust the Bible much more! However, there is something to be said for having an agreed-upon definition of terms.

Have you ever had a conversation with someone and assumed you were both talking about the same thing? Later, you found out you weren't even close? When our kids were younger, we would have a Spanish word for the week, and sometimes we would attend our church's Spanish ministry to provide some extra exposure along with language / culture immersion.

On one particular week, we were learning the word *pescado*, a word that means <u>fish</u>. We would try to use it in sentences, etc. It's a fairly innocent word with no theological implications – or so we thought! We were about to have that thought tested!

That Sunday we went to the Spanish service and the speaker spoke *rapidamente!* We were only catching a few words here and there. But there was at least one word our kids definitely recognized (or so they thought!). After the service, they wanted to know why the Spanish pastor was on a rant against fish!

This led to a comical exchange as we tried to explain to our kids that *fish* hadn't been the thrust of the sermon. The preacher had not been saying *pescado*; he had been saying *pecado*. Yep, sounds very similar…means nothing alike! That week, our kids learned an extra word: *pecado* – sin! They weren't on the same page at all!

The illustration above is humorous – we still laugh about it on occasion. But it's no laughing matter when the context moves from *pecado / pescado* to the subjects of sin and doctrine. Imagine now that you are asking this question to someone from the Mormon religion, "Do you believe Jesus is the Son of God?" The answer you will receive is "Yes."

As you continue the conversation, perhaps you ask, "Do you believe Jesus died for your sins?" Again, the answer will be "Yes."

The problem isn't the answer – it's the definition and understanding of what is being answered.

In Christianity, to say that Jesus is the Son of God is to recognize Him as God. Mormons do not believe that Jesus is God. They believe He is the Son of Elohim through a relationship with a human mother.

Again, in Christianity, to affirm that Jesus died for our sins is to affirm that the sin debt has been paid. In Mormon theology, the affirmation carries the idea that our sin debt has been refinanced – and we have all of eternity to work off that debt to Jesus.

In our fictitious conversation, we could easily believe that two very different theologies are aligned – when in fact, they are worlds apart. If you don't define terms, you will just keep speaking in circles. The same is true with this subject of dispensationalism.

Definitions aren't just important in the realm of theology. In a book that deals with argumentation and debate, two writers treat that age-old question: "If a tree falls in a forest, but nobody hears it – did it make a sound?"

The answer to the question is dependent solely upon your definition of *sound*. If it is defined as waves in the air, the answer is given in the affirmative. If *sound* is defined as the subjective experience of hearing, it's answered in the negative. How can a simple question – a yes or no question – be answered with both words? It's all in the definitions![7]

In Charles Ryrie's classic book, *Dispensationalism*, he opens with these memorable words: "The mention of the word

---

[7] Austin J. Freeley and David L. Steinberg, *Argumentation and Debate: Critical Thinking for Reasoned Decision Making* (Wadsworth CENGAGE Learning, 2009), 63.

dispensationalism usually evokes an immediate reaction."[8] Fewer words have been more accurately given. I have had the privilege to teach and discuss the concepts of dispensational theology in the college classroom for many years. Regardless of the generation represented by the students entering the class, the facial expressions have always been the same – fear!

For some students, it is the fear of the unknown. They've never heard the word *dispensationalism* used before (though most of them have been exposed to dispensational hermeneutics). For other students, it's the fear of the work ("Oh, that's the class with the major research project?!"). Regardless of their background, the mention of the word *dispensationalism* evokes an immediate reaction.

I've also enjoyed discussing dispensational concepts with non-dispensationalists. When I mention that I am a dispensationalist, the reactions are

KEY CONCEPT

A person in authority dispenses responsibilities to another – and then holds them accountable for those responsibilities.

mixed. They run from disbelief, to shock, to silence, and to those who want to help me see the light. Yes, I believe Ryrie's words were accurate – mention dispensationalism and watch the reactions. But remember, sometimes the reaction comes because what a person *thinks* dispensationalism is doesn't align with what it *actually* is.

---

[8] Charles Ryrie, *Dispensationalism* (Chicago: Moody, 1995), 11.

Defining Dispensation

At the root of dispensationalism is this word *dispense* or *dispensation*. In our vernacular, when we *dispense* something, we are distributing something to someone. Teachers dispense knowledge. Parents dispense money! But also embedded into this concept is the idea of distributing / dispensing with accountability set in. In other words, think of it in terms of one in authority dispensing responsibilities to someone under them – and then holding them accountable to their responsibilities.

In biblical times, the wealthier homes would have a hired servant who was given the responsibility to tend to the education of the children, the affairs of the home, and other daily activities. He was called a *steward*.[9] While thoughts within dispensationalism can apply to times or periods, the emphasis is more on the responsibility – the stewardship of which we give an account.

Elements not for sale

In Ryrie's (as well as others') book, the concept of *sine qua non*, a Latin phrase meaning *essentials*, comes up.

Dispensationalists do not have to swear on Scofield's grave. They don't have to believe in seven dispensations or face the wrath of all others.

---

[9] In 1 Cor 4.2, Paul says faithfulness is required in *stewards*. The word he uses is the plural form of οικονομος (oikonomos). Remember this word – you'll see it again. When you do, remember that the concept of stewardship is an important element within dispensational theology.

They have flexibility to be non-Calvinistic or Calvinistic, or other mediating positions. They can believe the church benefits from the New Covenant or it doesn't - and still be a dispensationalist! They are not tied to one Bible translation.

ESSENTIALS

1. A normal, historical-grammatical hermeneutic

2. A distinction between Israel and the church

3. God's glory is the unifying purpose for history

However, there are three elements that are the sacred cows - touch these and you die! Well, maybe not that severe, but if you don't abide by these, your commitment to dispensationalism is questioned. The first non-negotiable, the hermeneutics, is foundational. Then, the other two, a distinction between Israel and the church as well as a doxological purpose, are natural outgrowths from this.

The Hermeneutics[10]

The first non-negotiable is a recognition that a commitment to the practice of consistent, normal, literal, <u>historical-grammatical method</u> of Bible interpretation is mandatory. This is our

---

[10] Remember, this is a term that deals with the art and science of biblical interpretation.

hermeneutical approach. It's not for sale. It's not a method to use when it provides the meaning we want. It is *the* method.

In the sports world, these non-negotiables might be understood as the fundamentals of the game. In baseball, you may have athletes with differing skill sets, but there is one non-negotiable to always remember. Frankly, it doesn't matter whether you are on offense or defense – the principle is the same. "Keep your eye on the ball!" That's non-negotiable. Once you are on the team, you can improve in other areas – but this non-negotiable is the entry point. If you're not willing to watch the ball, don't try out.

In similar fashion, there are areas of Bible study we can improve with time and with experience. But, we don't even get to consider ourselves a dispensationalist until we understand this first non-negotiable. A dispensationalist is committed to the literal, historical, grammatical method of understanding Scripture. This is *the* method!

The word *literal* is misleading, so dispensationalists sometimes use the word "normal" or "plain." The word *normal* is sometimes offensive because it can imply that anyone who uses a different approach is abnormal. The word "plain" simply means we look for a common-sense meaning. Obviously, biblical writers used figures of speech - just like we do today. When I say "I'm going to run to the store..." – no one takes me *literally*. The common-sense approach is that I am *going* to the store.

I've noticed that I am sometimes not even aware of the colloquialisms I use until I am in a foreign country preaching through an interpreter. Once in El Salvador, it was raining with great force. The rain bouncing off the metal roof made it difficult to hear. In the middle of my sermon, I said, "Wow, it's raining cats and dogs here!"

My interpreter stopped and said, "I can't say that..." Ever the encourager, I assured him that he could. I even supplied the words for him: *los gatos* (cats) and *los perros* (dogs). He reminded me that he knew how to translate cats and dogs; that wasn't the problem. Rather, the problem was that a word-for-word translation from English to Spanish would have been nonsense to the audience. Instead, he said something like it was raining buckets…He gave the common-sense meaning of my poorly chosen words.

Therefore, when John quotes Jesus as saying, "I am the Door…" – no one believes Jesus is made of wood, has hinges, and is waiting to spring open to let us in. It's a figure of speech that plainly tells us that He is the way to God. So, because of this approach, dispensationalists take Scripture at face-value.

Consider the context of prophecy. This is an area where dispensationalists and non-dispensationalists disagree. Writing in a commentary about Ezekiel, Cooper provides this description:

> Premillennialism is the teaching that Christ's second coming will inaugurate a visible kingdom of righteousness that will comprise the whole earth. The term "dispensationalism" refers to a system of scriptural interpretation that stresses literal fulfillment of prophecy as well as distinctions in God's administrative program historically, that is, "dispensations."[11]

Dispensationalists see a future for Israel because that's a plain reading of the text. Non-dispensationalists see those prophecies as spiritually fulfilled in the church. This isn't a question of, "Who loves Jesus more?" This isn't even a question of, "Which Bible should I use?" Rather, this is a question with, "How do I interpret the Bible?"

---

[11] Lamar Eugene Cooper, *Ezekiel*, vol. 17, The New American Commentary (Nashville: Broadman & Holman Publishers, 1994), 45.

Here's the problem with inconsistent hermeneutics. When the Old Testament prophesies that Jesus would be born in Bethlehem – that's where He was literally born (not spiritually, but physically). When the Old Testament predicts that He would rise from the dead – He did that literally. In fact, all the prophecies that are already fulfilled have been *literally* fulfilled. So, dispensationalists believe there is a **biblical** precedent for interpreting the Scriptures literally.[12]

It is also worth mentioning that there is a **logical** reason for interpreting Scriptures this way as well. God created language for communication. God desires to communicate to man and to hold him accountable for what he does with that communication. If all of the Old Testament prophecies were meant to be fulfilled spiritually, God did not communicate clearly to the Old Testament believers.

Three Reasons for Normal Interpretation

1. Biblical
2. Logical
3. Hermeneutical

Further, we have a **hermeneutical** reason for using this approach. If someone uses a less-than-literal approach to the text, they are now sliding into subjectivity on the textual meaning. A

---

[12] A dispensational approach attempts to remove subjectivity. It is not up to the reader to decide this prophecy is fulfilled literally. This one is fulfilled spiritually, etc. Rather, a dispensationalist uses the same method consistently.

normal, plain-sense, historical-grammatical approach allows us to be as objective as possible in saying, "This is what the text means."

Despite the biblical and logical reasons for utilizing this approach as well as the benefit of more objectivity, fairness demands that we notate some potential weaknesses in this method as well. There is some "in-house" debate on whether hermeneutics includes application of the text to our present day. Is hermeneutics solely interested in what the text *meant* or does it include the text's *significance* for today?

For those who have sat in my classes, I love to introduce a tool called the hermeneutical circle (see the appendix). After working through the biblical, historical, and systematic theologies, I believe the interpreter's task isn't finished until he handles the practical theology. So, I would be one of those who say application should be part of our understanding of the text.

What does any of this have to do with dispensationalism's hermeneutical approach? Frankly, if we emphasize the historical-grammatical context *only*, we may develop a blind spot that doesn't allow us to bridge the gap from then to now. This isn't a death-knell for the historical-grammatical method; it just means we need to be aware of a potential weakness in our explanation of the text.

A second weakness – and this is true of *all* hermeneutical methods – is that we never fully disengage our presuppositions. What this means, in practical terms, is that while we are doing our best to be objective with the text, we may have blind spots where our theology is driving our exegesis.[13] This is why all biblical expositors

---

[13] This word may not be familiar for some. It means "to pull out of" and in the context of hermeneutics, it simply means the meaning is pulled from the text. The opposite of this is eisegesis, which means "to put in" and has the idea of reading the interpreter's meaning into the text.

have to come to the text with humility and confess our own weakness as sinful people.

At the end of the day, here's the rub. Dispensationalism is more than a *system* – though I'm not opposed to calling it that. More accurately, however, it is the result – the fruit – of a consistent commitment to a normal, plain, historical-grammatical approach to interpretation. While covenant theology would maintain this same approach for most of the Scriptures, dispensationalism maintains this approach even in the prophetic sections.[14]

Two Distinct Entities

The second non-negotiable is that dispensationalists observe a <u>distinction between Israel and the Church</u>. While all believers will come together in eternity, in this thing called "time," God is working with His stewards. His steward, Israel, has been temporarily set aside due to their hardness of heart and rejection of her King. Currently, God is working through His church. But, one day, after the church is called to heaven, God will once again begin working through Israel to reach this world.

The church has a different **character** than the nation of Israel. The Old Testament nation was comprised of the physical descendants of Abraham, Isaac, and Jacob. They were given a physical land by inheritance. To these people were given the rite of circumcision as well as the Mosaic Covenant.

The church, however, is different. It is made up of "red, yellow, black and white." In the church are Jews and Gentiles,

---

[14] Consequently, a dispensationalist cannot take a prophecy made specifically to the nation of Israel and have it fulfilled in the church. Covenant theology will be defined more fully later.

together in one body. The church is not a nation and has no physical land by inheritance. The character / make-up is different.

More importantly, the church is distinct from Israel in its **timing**. The nation of Israel is officially brought into a covenant relationship at the first Pentecost in the Old Testament. Fifty days after leaving Egypt (Passover), the nation is at Mount Sinai receiving the law, the Mosaic Covenant.

Interestingly, after the ultimate Passover where God's Lamb was slain once, for all, and forever, we come to another historic Pentecost. At the first Pentecost, the law was given. At this Pentecost, the Spirit was given.[15] At that first Pentecost, a new entity - a nation bound in covenant to Jehovah - was formed. At this Pentecost, another new entity was

The Church and Israel

Different in CHARACTER

Different in TIMING

formed - the Bride of Christ, the Body of Christ - the Church.

Paul makes a set of important distinctions while writing to the church at Corinth. In 1 Corinthians 10.32, Paul instructs the Corinthians to give no offense. Specifically, he warns them not to offend the *Jews*, the *Gentiles*, nor the *Church of God*. The Gentiles were not synonymous with the church of God. Neither were the Jews. There are three separate entities referenced here.

According to Paul's teaching in Ephesians 3 and Colossians 1, the church was a *mystery* in the Old Testament. It was neither revealed nor known. It was not revealed until the Messiah-King first

---

[15] For more, see Eddie Chumney, *The Seven Festivals of the Messiah*, specifically chapter 6. Http://hebroots.com/sevenfestivals_chap6.htm.

offered the kingdom to Israel. Upon their rejection and His crucifixion, God's mysterious agent, the Church, was revealed, formed, organized, and commissioned to spread the gospel.

God's Purpose

The third non-negotiable is understanding that <u>God's central purpose in all He does is doxological</u> (a term that refers to His glory). Some systems have as its central core the Person of Christ - a Christological center. That's a great center, but does it encompass all that God does?

Others have our salvation as central - a soteriological center. Again, that's an important issue. But does it encompass all that God does? Some speak of being gospel-centered, covenant-centered, and even biblio-centric. Do these centers, as important as they are, put all the pieces into proper relationship with each other?

Consider that God made countless planets and stars. Why? The angelic world, animal kingdom, and plant life are all under His control. For what purpose? We will not share the gospel in eternity. But we will praise God and bring glory to Him. Dispensationalists see the unifying center of what God does to be centered on His glory - a doxological center.

God's preeminent purpose throughout all ages has been to glorify Himself. This principle is the primary unifier for all ages. While His plan of redemption is without equal, it is only one means by which He glorifies Himself. The way God deals with the saved, with the unsaved, with the angels, with the fallen angels, and with all of His creation ultimately revolves around His glory.

Defining Dispensationalism

Many definitions have been set forth for dispensationalism - some helpful and others not so much. One definition offered often is this one: "**A dispensation is a distinguishable economy in the outworking of God's purpose.**"[16] Great…But what does *that* even mean? What makes it *distinguishable*? What is an *economy*? When people hear the word *economy* today, it's usually not in a theological context. When our definitions need defining, we've probably made it too complicated.

ECONOMY

In this context, it refers to the administration, rule, and management of a household.

Did you have a high school English teacher that loved etymology? I did! I didn't enjoy it always at the moment, but I am grateful for the experience today. Because of a rudimentary understanding and interest of where words come from, Ryrie's use of "economy" makes sense to me. But without the background information, I would probably be confused.

Next time you are shopping for Greek yogurt, look for the brand *Oikos*. It's a Greek word, that means "house." It's a word that is found in our New Testament. In our Bibles, the word is also used as a compound part with a second word, "nomos." So, the word *oikonomos* is used in the New Testament and is traditionally translated as "steward."

---

[16] Ryrie, *Dispensationalism*, 28.

Don't get "lost in translation!" You have already seen the word "nomos" before. It's part of one of our Old Testament books, Deutero-nomy (*deuteros-nomos*). The word *nomos* deals with "laws and managing." You've probably seen it in the word *autonomy / autonomous* (*autos-nomos*). So, *oikonomos*, in a simple definition would be a "house-law." It deals with the steward who administers / orders the affairs of the house according to the master's command.

Great - what does all of this have to do with Ryrie? Well, the Greek word *oikonomos | oikonomia* is brought into the Latin language as *oeconomia*, where it is brought into the English language as – you guessed it – *economy*. In its context, the word *economy* deals with the administration, the rule, and management of a household. This is a key thought. Built into the woof and fabric of dispensationalism is that of stewardship and accountability.

Renald Showers offers this insight by defining the term *dispensation* as it relates to Dispensational Theology as "a particular way of God's <u>administering His rule</u> [which comes from understanding the context of Ryrie's word *economy*] over the world as He progressively works out His purpose for world history."[17] This is a helpful definition as it focuses on God's administration of and God's progressive revelation to the world He has created.

The understanding of God's rule being administered differently throughout history was observed by John Calvin (before the systems of Covenant Theology and Dispensational Theology were fully developed):

> If a farmer sets certain tasks for his household in the winter, other tasks for the summer, we shall not on this account accuse him of inconstancy, or think that he departs from the proper rule of

---

[17] Renald Showers, An Introduction to Dispensational Theology. http://gracebiblestudies.org/resources/Web.

agriculture, which accords with the continuous order of nature. In like manner, if a householder instructs, rules, and guides his children one way in infancy, another way in youth, and still another in young manhood, we shall not on this account call him fickle and say that he abandons his purpose. Why, then, do we brand God with the mark of inconstancy because he has with apt and fitting marks distinguished a diversity of times?[18]

Obviously, Calvin would not be a dispensationalist. Perhaps some of his followers would even object to me using his words in this context. Yet, the truth remains that the analogy he uses is spot-on for describing the way God administers his rule over his household.

The Oxford Dictionary, in defining *dispensationalism*, uses the following: "A belief in a system of historical progression, as revealed in the Bible, consisting of a series of stages in God's self-revelation and plan of salvation."[19] Dispensationalism is a system and, as Oxford has noted, this system is revealed in the Bible.

In Vlach's book, *Dispensationalism: Essential Beliefs and Common Myths*, he devotes a chapter for common questions. The first question asks what would be a good, short definition of dispensationalism. Here was his response:

> Dispensationalism is a system of theology primarily concerned with the doctrines of ecclesiology and eschatology that emphasizes applying historical-grammatical hermeneutics to all passages of Scripture (including the entire Old Testament). It affirms a distinction between Israel and the church, and a future salvation and restoration of the nation Israel in a future earthly kingdom

---

[18] John Calvin, *Institutes of the Christian Religion* (London: Wolfe and Harison, 1561), II:XI:13.

[19] Definition at http://lexico.com/en/definition/dispensationalism.

under Jesus the Messiah as the basis for a worldwide kingdom that brings blessings to all nations.[20]

Matt Slick defines dispensationalism as "an approach to biblical interpretation which states that God uses different means of working with people (Israel and the church) during different periods of history."[21] He has correctly noted that dispensationalism is connected to one's hermeneutics – it's an approach to biblical interpretation.

Every definition has its limitations. We typically attempt to offer a pithy definition to encapsulate an entire system. Ultimately, however, important concepts are sacrificed for the sake of brevity. Yet, knowing the inherent limitations in definitions, here is the definition I use: *Dispensationalism is a system of historical progression consisting of a series of stages in God's self-revelation to man, anchored by a historical-grammatical hermeneutic which results in a distinction between Israel and the Church and which also unifies progressive revelation around a doxological purpose.*

Yes – I ask my students to memorize this definition! I wish it were shorter – but there is nothing within this definition that I want to sacrifice. I have attempted to choose *clarity* over *brevity*. While it may seem like a mouthful, the definition contains key phrases that are important to this conversation.

---

[20] Michael Vlach, *Dispensationalism: Essential Beliefs and Common Myths* (Los Angeles: Theological Studies Press, 2008), 93.

[21] Matt Slick, "What is Dispensationalism?" CARM, https://carm.org/dispensationalism.

Dispensationalism is a System

In breaking down this definition, notice that dispensationalism is a "system." A system implies a framework that is unified based upon a set of principles. It provides a method for doing one's work. In this sense, Dispensationalism is a system that is vitally connected to our hermeneutics (how we interpret and understand the Bible).

Dispensationalism is not the only system available. Covenant Theology is a competing system for theologians. Showers provides a simple definition for covenant theology in his work, *There Really is a Difference*. He defined it as a theological system that develops the Bible's philosophy of history on the basis of a few covenants. Basically, it represents the Scripture *en toto* and history as being covered by two or three covenants.[22]

Other theological systems would include Arminianism / Wesleyanism contrasted with Calvinism. Liberation theology and feminist theology present outliers to the typical conservative evangelical. Other theologies emphasize promise or kingdom. Dispensationalism and covenant theology remain the most popular options and are often contrasted with each other because of this.

The importance of progressive revelation

Secondly, this definition hones in on the idea of God's progressive revelation. This is vitally important to understand because it has great bearing on how we interpret Scriptures (or, how we "rightly divide" the Word of truth - 1 Timothy 2.15). Consider the following:

Adam never read the Bible! No, that's not the reason he sinned!

---

[22] Renald E. Showers, *There Really Is a Difference! A Comparison of Covenant and Dispensational Theology* (Bellmawr, NJ: The Friends of Israel Gospel Ministry, Inc., 1990), 7.

Abraham couldn't recite the Ten Commandments...not one!
David did not love his enemies. Imprecatory Psalms, anyone?
John the Baptist never preached about the Rapture.
Paul didn't know about the Seven Trumpet Judgments.

Why is this so? At the core of this discussion is the concept of progressive revelation. God gave truth to man – revelation to man – here a little, there a little. It was line upon line, precept upon precept. Thus, we cannot judge David by New Testament standards. We cannot judge Jacob according to the Mosaic Covenant.

The Bible characters were responsible to live according to the truth that had been given *up through their time*. We can't assume that the Bible characters had access to the same amount of truth we have.

As simple as the truth above may be, it has direct bearing on biblical interpretation. As we are reading and interpreting a text, certain questions need to be asked. What revelation had been given to that point? How would they have understood the instructions in their historical context?

Every person has presuppositions - blind spots in his theology. I'm no exception. In my mind, my hermeneutic makes perfect sense – I struggle to see why others reject it! Yet, I know there are people within covenantalism that feel the same way about their theology – and wonder why I don't get it! Part of my bias is linked to the priority of the testaments.

When I read something in the Old Testament, my first response isn't to look for a link to the New Testament. I start with what would have been understood by that audience. This leads us to a third element of our working definition.

Normal, historical-grammatical hermeneutic

Thirdly, this definition emphasizes the core essential to dispensationalism - the normal, historical-grammatical hermeneutic.

As briefly alluded to already, the Bible has a *historical* context. A dispensationalist understands that the Bible has a unified theme – yet, he also understands that it wasn't given all at one time. So, in our interpretation of a passage, we want to understand the historical setting. What revelation has been given? Who is the audience? What is the purpose for the book?

Additionally, the *grammatical* context is considered. Is this a command, a principle, a narrative, a rhetorical question, a figure of speech? William Tolar shares a story when a King of England went to visit St. Paul's Cathedral in London. The Cathedral is impressive, having been designed by the famous Christopher Wren. By all historical accounts, and even by today's standards – the place is a masterpiece.

Do you know what the King said about the cathedral? He said it was "awful" and "artificial." In our day, those words are insulting. In *that* day, they were highly complimentary. As Tolar explains,

> "Awful" meant "full of awe" and "artificial" meant "artistic in the superlative degree." Words have meanings, but these can change with time and context. To understand any language, whether spoken or written, one must begin with the meanings of words as they were intended by the original author.[23]

Christopher Cone observes several key results, or benefits, of consistently setting the Scriptures in their historical and grammatical context. First, the interpreter demonstrates submission to the

---

[23] Bruce Corley, Steve Lemke, and Grant Lovejoy, *Biblical Hermeneutics: A Comprehensive Introduction to Interpreting Scripture*, 2nd ed. (Nashville, TN: Broadman & Holman, 2002), 22.

authority of Scripture.[24] Further, the interpreter is able to recognize both progressive and cumulative revelation.

Showers explains that dispensationalism is "convinced that the historical-grammatical method should be employed for all of Scripture, including those prophetic passages related to Israel and the Kingdom of God."[25] This method of Bible interpretation is a key component within dispensationalism and is the foundation for the entire system.

According to Robert Utley, there are three guiding principles to summarize this approach to hermeneutics: 1) The Bible was written in normal language. 2) The Bible must be interpreted in light of its historical context. 3) The original intent of the writer must be the focal point of interpretation.[26] I'm not sure who said it, but it's accurate - "It cannot mean what it never meant!"

Let's see this in practice. In Psalm 22, David writes, "My God, my God - why have you forsaken me?" Dispensationalists are well aware that Jesus quotes this while on the cross. Yet, that is not the beginning of the exegesis for Psalm 22. When a dispensationalist reads Psalm 22, he starts with this question: "Why would David say this? Why would a believer feel this way?" After developing the historical meaning, the question David asked can be asked by others in succeeding generations - including Jesus. Yet, Jesus' use of Psalm 22 doesn't change the original meaning.

---

[24] Christopher Cone, *Prolegomena on Biblical Hermeneutics and Method*, 2nd Edition. (Hurst, TX: Tyndale Seminary Press, 2012), 156.

[25] Renald Showers, *There Really is a Difference! A Comparison of Covenant and Dispensational Theology* (Bellmawr, NJ: The Friends of Israel Gospel Ministry, 1990).

[26] Robert James Utley, *You Can Understand the Bible!* (Marshall, TX: Bible Lessons International, 1996), 26.

What is important to note is that a dispensationalist doesn't read Psalm 22 and teach that it's meaning can only be discovered by looking to the cross. In contrast to a dispensational understanding of Scriptures, those who embrace Covenant Theology often give priority to the New Testament.

Keep in mind that two people, reading the same Bible, come to different conclusions based on how they approach the text. For a dispensationalist, with his emphasis upon progressive revelation and an historical-grammatical hermeneutic, he will read the Old Testament and start there for its meaning. Not every believer begins with that presupposition. Some believers start with the full understanding of New Testament revelation and read that back into the Old Testament.

Is allowing the New Testament to have priority a problem? It doesn't have to be – but there is an inherent danger. When the Old Testament is interpreted through the lens of the New Testament (rather than its own historical context), it's possible to change the original meaning of the text. Again, it cannot mean what it never meant.

A doxological purpose

Back to the definition supplied for dispensationalism, this hermeneutic will lead one to two inescapable conclusions: 1) God has a distinct plan for Israel and for the church - these two entities are not identical. 2) God does everything He does - and all of Holy Scripture concurs - for His glory (this is the meaning of *doxological*).

When a dispensationalist states that doxology is a distinctive of his system, this can sound arrogant. After all, reformed and covenant theologians embrace whole-heartedly the glory of God. We shouldn't imply that dispensationalists are the only ones left who believe God does everything for His glory – that would be untrue and a ridiculous (and indefensible) statement.

So, what do we mean? We have roughly 6,000 years of human history, sixty-six inspired books, and all of eternity in which the works and ways of God are manifested. How do we organize all of that information? Is there a way to bring an over-arching unifying principle? It is within this context that dispensationalists offer the principle of God's glory.

Some systems place a heavy emphasis on salvation. That's an important doctrine and worthy of much discussion. But, can we unify all of history and eternity around this theme? Why did God create animals, plants, trees, and angels? Salvation becomes too narrow to encompass these other concepts.

These same questions pose difficulty for those who seek to make *kingdom* or *promise* their unifying principle. Dispensationalists believe that a doxological purpose is central to all that God does or will do.

Why did God create angels? For His glory. Why are there animals, plants, and trees? For His glory. Why will God judge the wicked and reward the righteous? For His glory. Why did God create angels when humans are the ones with whom He will reign? Why did God create man when He already had angels? Regardless of the question, the answer remains the same – His glory.

Starting Point for Hermeneutics

The art and science of hermeneutics, unfortunately, isn't as simple as opening a passage and saying, "This text means…" In this field, much is happening in the background. Presuppositions formed by our theological systems, favorite preachers, churches we attend, etc, all have some bearing on what we "see" in the text.

Sometimes in this conversation, new terms like *continuity* and *discontinuity* get bandied about as well. John Feinberg edited an entire book entitled, *Continuity and Discontinuity: Perspectives on the Relationship Between the Old and New Testaments.*[27] But what does this even mean?

In the context of this discussion, continuity seeks to find a continuous theme from the Old Testament to the New Testament. Those on the continuity side find only one people of God - there is no distinction between the church and Israel. The terminology that describes the continuity side runs the full spectrum - from the church being the *replacement* for Israel, to the church being the *fulfillment* of the Old Testament prophecies.

Theologians who skew toward continuity have no qualms of discussing the church in the Old Testament or finding Israel in the New Testament. Hear a representative quote from this perspective:

> Nowhere in the NT is the church described as "true Israel," "real Israel," "spiritual Israel," "new Israel," "renewed Israel," or the like. And, with the exception of Galatians 6:16 and Revelation 7:4, nowhere is the name "Israel" applied directly to the church. However, is it incorrect to speak of the church as "Israel"? The answer is "No." We may speak correctly of the church as "Israel" in this accommodative way because of the many images of Israel found in the New Testament which are applied to the church.[28]

---

[27] John Feinberg. Editor, *Continuity and Discontinuity: Perspectives on the Relationship Between the Old and New Testaments* (Westchester, IL: Crossway Books, 1988).

[28] Chris Reeves, "The People of God: A Study of the Continuity and Discontinuity Between OT Israel and the NT Church." He adds a footnote giving approval to those who refer to the church as "spiritual Israel." Read his article: https://thegoodteacher.com/Special/The%20People%20of%20God%20(Reeves).pdf.

Discontinuity sees a different plan unfolding in the New Testament. Previously, God had worked through His people, the nation of Israel. Now, He is working through a different group - the local church. The closer one leans toward discontinuity, the more they fall on the spectrum of dispensational theology.

At the core of whether one leans to discontinuity or continuity is their starting point for their hermeneutical method. Merkle wrestles with the fact that both systems affirm a historical-grammatical interpretation, so why the differences? His conclusion is that the issue is the priority given to either the Old or New Testament.[29] Herbert Bateman explains, "Testament priority is a presuppositional preference of one testament over the other that determines a person's literal historical-grammatical hermeneutical starting point."[30]

Generally speaking, dispensationalists will land on the discontinuity side and covenantalists will land on the continuity side. Generally speaking, dispensationalists will begin their historical-grammatical approach beginning with the Old Testament and progressing forward. Generally speaking, covenantalists will begin their approach affirming the priority of the New Testament and reading it backwards. From a dispensational viewpoint, this approach offers contradictory or changing meanings of the text.

These are complex issues and outside the scope of this book. However, the fact that these complexities exist demonstrates the

---

[29] Benjamin Merkley, *Discontinuity to Continuity: A Survey of Dispensational and Covenantal Theologies* (Bellingham: Lexham, 2020), 8.

[30] Herbert Bateman, *Three Central Issues in Contemporary Dispensationalism* (Grand Rapids, MI: Kregel, 1999), 38.

importance of understanding that real differences occur between systems of interpretation.

Summary

Terms are important and must be defined. We have a working definition of dispensationalism that we can use moving forward. We have also high-lighted these important terms:

1. *Hermeneutics* - a term used to describe the branch of knowledge that deals with biblical interpretation. It is both an art and a skill.

2. *Historical-Grammatical* - this is the hermeneutic approach used by dispensationalists. The goal is to understand a passage in its historical context (rather than reading our modern-day context into it) as well as its grammatical context. In short, it begins with this question, "How would the original hearers have understood this passage?"

3. *Progressive Revelation* - While the term is self-explanatory, dispensationalism reminds its adherents that to interpret David's actions based upon New Testament principles is illogical - he didn't have the New Testament. That revelation that God gave was given progressively...here a little, there a little.

4. *Oikonomia* - a strange Greek word that perhaps we've never heard, but will remember every time we buy Greek yogurt. The picture painted by this word is one of a steward, a house manager, ruling the affairs of the house. In dispensational thought, God has governed His house by *dispensing* different responsibilities throughout history.

5. *Doxological* - Dispensationalists center God's revelation and purpose around the theme of God's glory (doxa). This theme is broad enough to include His plans for the angels, for the animal kingdom, etc. While salvation is an important theme, God's purpose throughout all of eternity encompasses more.

6. *Continuity* - Continuity is defined as the "unbroken and consistent existence or operation of something over a period of time." In this view, the "church" was in the Old Testament, and the church is the "spiritual Israel" today - one people of God, continuously, between both testaments.

7. *Discontinuity* – In contrast to continuity, this emphasizes a sharp distinction between two options. Those who hold this view do NOT see the church in the Old Testament and the church is NOT the New (or spiritual) Israel.

Chapter 2

HISTORICAL CONTEXT

*Those who don't understand history
are like trees without roots*

"If one does not bring a lamb to the altar in worshiping God, then he is a dispensationalist. One who worships on Sunday instead of Saturday is also a dispensationalist, because he recognizes the Sabbath was for Israel, not the church."[31] - Lewis Sperry Chafer

Chapter Aims

1. You will understand some of the historical background from which dispensationalism has grown.
2. You will understand that dispensational thought (not a systematized theology) can trace its history to the early church.
3. You will understand that while John Darby was influential in many respects, American Dispensationalism was notably different in key areas.
4. You will understand that no theological system sits above the God-inspired text.

---

[31] Paul Enns, *Handbook of Theology* (Chicago: Moody, 1989), 520.

Introduction

Do you remember those age-old, philosophical questions that we learned to think about in school? I'm talking about those questions that show humanity's attempt to find meaning and purpose? Who/what am I? Where did I come from? Where am I going? Well, these questions can also apply to dispensationalism. Since we defined dispensationalism and its key terms in the last chapter, we're ready to undertake this historical investigation.

In this chapter, we are interested in finding out from where dispensationalism came. Those who oppose dispensationalism sometimes argue that it is a recent invention – thus, not worthy of our consideration. Consider Harbach's strongly worded assessment:

> ...Dispensationalism is a questionable hermeneutical method relatively new, arising as it did in England and Ireland about 136 years ago, its ideas were in some places prevalent 280 years ago.[32]

Harbach takes issue with the hermeneutical approach of dispensationalism. Writing in 1967, he attempts to be charitable by allowing a time lapse of 280 years for some of this thinking. But still, it's clear in reading Harbach that the ancient church had a different hermeneutic from today's dispensationalism. Stated another way, in his mind, dispensationalism is a *departure* or *deviation* from the hermeneutics of the early church.

---

[32] Robert Harbach, "Dispensationalism: An Ancient Error." 1967. Protestant Reformed Churches in America. http://www.prca.org/resources/publications/articles/item/3741-dispensationalism-an-ancient-error.

Dispensationalism is a theological, hermeneutical system that is utilized in understanding God's message communicated through the Scriptures. As a full-blown systematized approach to understanding God's revelation, it is relatively new. Harbach's assertion is true. Yet, I do not mean to imply that dispensational thoughts and concepts are new (which is a common argument against the validity of dispensationalism). Rather, it is an attempt to objectively state that the *system* taught here developed over time.

> ## Key Question
> *Hermeneutics of dispensationalism: A **development** or a **departure** from the hermeneutics of the early church?*

So, before we dive into the nuts and bolts of dispensationalism, explaining what it is, let's take a look at the historical context in which dispensationalism finds its roots, explaining where it came from (and how it developed). A friendly warning for the remainder of this chapter: If history "isn't your thing," bear with me for at least a chapter!

Early Dispensational Thought

It's not uncommon for detractors of dispensationalism to assert that these thoughts originated in the late 1800s. Yet, quite the opposite is true. In fairness, however, we should note that dispensationalism – as a full-blown, mature theological system – cannot be found in the early church. That's not what we are looking for. We are looking for (and I believe we find) the seeds that would grow into this system. As a result of this search, we should conclude that these seeds were very much present.

By the way, a system's validity shouldn't be measured by time alone or by who said this or that – it should be judged based on its fidelity to the Scriptures. As students of church history already understand, different periods in church history witnessed the church battling various doctrinal issues.

At times, the church was involved in *Christological* heresies and at other times *canonical* issues. Yet, at other times, the church was focused on Trinitarian debates. Dispensationalism has a strong emphasis on eschatology, a study that was slower in developing in a systematized way.[33]

Before taking a whirl-wind tour through history to "prove" the validity of a system that we just confessed wasn't developed until the 1800s, it might be helpful to know what we are looking for. Some of the seeds for what would become known as dispensationalism include the following:

1. A dependency upon a consistent historical-grammatical approach to understanding the text as opposed to an allegorical, spiritual approach to understanding the text.

2. A recognition that the church is a distinct group of believers that is separate from the nation of Israel.

3. An eschatology that anticipates Jesus taking His church to Heaven *before* the time of tribulation at the end.

One of the more vocal opponents to dispensationalism, and especially the pre-tribulational rapture of the church, is David MacPherson. Because of dispensationalism's commitment to its

---

[33] This makes sense. The early church wasn't interested in hundreds or thousands of years of prophetic truth. From their perspective, Jesus was returning soon. When it became evident that no one could predict the time, matters of eschatology began to be studied in greater detail.

hermeneutics and its view that the church and Israel are distinct peoples – we typically hold a pre-tribulational rapture. The concepts of dispensational hermeneutics and our view of the timing of the rapture are not easily separated.

For MacPherson, his thesis is that during the first eighteen centuries of church history, no one separated the rapture from the Second Coming of Christ.[34] This two-stage coming (Rapture and then the second coming seven years later) was a recent invention. Usually, he credits the source for this view as being Margaret McDonald, a woman he views as being influenced by the occult. Thus, he attempts to discredit the [pre-tribulational] Rapture by appealing to a guilt by association fallacy.

Of course, MacPherson is not a lone voice. John Bray shares this same sentiment that no pre-tribulational position existed before the 1800s. He adamantly expresses that this was not a recovered truth once lost or neglected. Rather than being recovered or neglected, Bray believes this "truth" was invented. It was never taught by anyone.[35]

For people like Bray who object to a pre-tribulational rapture, they invite criticism when they assert that *no one* has **ever** taught pre-tribulationalism in 1800 years of church history. With such dogmatic statements, all it takes is for just *one person*, over a period of 1800 years, to disprove the allegation. Thomas Ice, a staunch defender of the pre-tribulational position, believes he has found just such a reference (and many more than just one reference).

---

[34] David MacPherson, *The Great Rapture Hoax* (Fletcher, NC: New Puritan Library, 1983), 15.

[35] John Bray, *The Origin of the Pre-Tribulation Rapture Teaching* (Lakeland, FL: self-published, 1982), 31-32.

Church leaders wrote often, leaving future generations a treasure trove of sermons, counsel, apologetics, etc. Many of these have been lost to antiquity – others are just now being rediscovered. One such manuscript is labeled as *Pseudo-Ephraim*. The dating is widely guessed to be between the early 300s to the middle of the 600s AD. Listen to this statement from a sermon entitled "On the Last Times, the Antichrist, and the End of the World."

> All the saints and elect of God are gathered together before the tribulation, which is to come, and are taken to the Lord, in order that they may not see at any time the confusion which overwhelms the world because of our sins.

Ice[36] does a scholarly job of setting the grammatical context of the sermon as well as the historical context of the pre-Islamic world. His conclusion – which is intellectually convincing – is that this is an early reference to a pre-tribulational rapture. If the dating is even remotely accurate, then this sermon was at least a thousand years *prior* to the 1800s.[37]

While post-millennialism (or amillennialism) became an entrenched position after Augustine, this was not always the case. Justin Martyr, one of the church's early apologists, laid out a dispensational view of premillennialism in his *Dialogue with Trypho* (written between 155-170 AD). In describing the future kingdom, Martyr states:

> "Of these and such like words written by the prophets, O Trypho, some have reference to the first advent of Christ, in

---

[36] Thomas Ice, "The Rapture in Pseudo-Ephraim," https://pretrib.org/pretribfiles/pdfs/Ice-TheRaptureinPseudo-Ephraem.pdf

[37] And in reality, it may have been even longer.

which He is preached as inglorious, obscure, and of mortal appearance: but others had reference to His second advent, when He shall appear in glory and above the clouds; and your nation shall see and know Him whom they have pierced, as Hosea, one of the twelve prophets, and Daniel, foretold."[38]

Justin, in his conversation with "Trypho the Jew" wants the Jewish skeptic to understand that the Messiah is coming again, He will be seen by Israel, and in the longer context of this passage, that He will establish their long-awaited kingdom. Premillennialism is the default position of dispensationalism (though, in fairness, post-tribulational Covenant Theologians also hold to a premillennial reign of Christ).

This is not a novel idea with Justin. In another work, *The First Apology,* Justin defends the need for a literal hermeneutic in the area of biblical prophecy – another hallmark of dispensationalism. Observe his words,

> Since, then, we prove that all things which have already happened had been predicted by the prophets before they came to pass, we must necessarily believe also that those things which are in like manner predicted, but are yet to come to pass, shall certainly happen.[39]

---

[38] Justin Martyr, "Dialogue of Justin with Trypho, a Jew," in *The Apostolic Fathers with Justin Martyr and Irenaeus*, ed. Alexander Roberts, James Donaldson, and A. Cleveland Coxe, vol. 1, The Ante-Nicene Fathers (Buffalo, NY: Christian Literature Company, 1885), 202.

[39] Justin Martyr, "The First Apology of Justin," in *The Apostolic Fathers with Justin Martyr and Irenaeus*, ed. Alexander Roberts, James Donaldson, and A. Cleveland Coxe, vol. 1, The Ante-Nicene Fathers (Buffalo, NY: Christian Literature Company, 1885), 180.

Note that he is arguing for a *literal* rather than a *symbolic* fulfillment for future prophecy. He doesn't expect the church to fulfill prophecies to Israel. He doesn't expect Revelation to be subjectively understood by assigning his own symbols. He is advocating a consistent dispensational hermeneutic. Irenaeus (120-202) handled prophecies in like manner:

> If, however, any shall endeavor to allegorize [prophecies] of this kind, they shall not be found consistent with themselves in all points, and shall be confuted by the teaching of the very expressions [in question].[40]

While Martyr and Irenaeus write early in church history, there is an even earlier witness to premillennial thought. Once again, we find a teaching rooted in a normal hermeneutical approach – this time coming from one of the disciples of the Apostle John.

Papias of Hierapolis (60-130AD) wrote volumes of works, mostly lost to history now. The Father of Ecclesiastical History, Eusebius (260-339AD) has preserved some of writings. While quoting Papias' belief in premillennial doctrine, Eusebius questions his intellect. Papias taught a millennium after the Resurrection - a belief that Eusebius attributed to his limited intelligence![41]

Could it be that Papias (and Irenaeus, his follower) held to premillennialism because that's what John taught? Could it be that

---

[40] Irenaeus of Lyons, "Irenæus against Heresies," in *The Apostolic Fathers with Justin Martyr and Irenaeus*, ed. Alexander Roberts, James Donaldson, and A. Cleveland Coxe, vol. 1, The Ante-Nicene Fathers (Buffalo, NY: Christian Literature Company, 1885), 565.

[41] Eusebius, *Ecclesiastical History*, iii.39.12.

they held these beliefs because that is what a normal hermeneutic would demand?

Eusebius argued that Revelation was symbolic and mystical, employing an allegorical approach to reading it. Would not these pre-Eusebian sources indicate that a literal hermeneutic was the normal approach before allegoricalism became popular?

Witness	Time Period
John the Apostle	6-100
Papias	60-130
Justin Martyr	100-170
Irenaeus	120-202
Nicene Council	325
Eusebius	*260-340*
Pseudo-Ephraim	300-600 (estimate)

Premillennial Views Held Prior to Eusebius

The point of these historical anecdotes is to help today's dispensationalist understand that his view of premillennialism is not new. As the noted historian, Philip Schaff, observed:

> The most striking point in the eschatology of the ante-Nicene age is the prominent chiliasm, or millenarianism.... It was indeed not the doctrine of the church embodied in any creed or form of devotion, but a widely current opinion of distinguished teachers."[42]

---

[42] Henry Clarence Thiessen and Vernon D. Doerksen, *Lectures in Systematic Theology* (Grand Rapids: Eerdmans, 1979), 365–366.

59

What one observes from church history is that early leaders advocated the same hermeneutic that today's dispensationalist insists upon. Because of that hermeneutic, there was a recognized distinction between Israel and the Church. Further, these early leaders held to a premillennialism that agreed with today's dispensationalism.

John Nelson Darby

The man oft credited as the Father of Dispensationalism is John Nelson Darby. In the book *131 Christians Everyone Should Know*, the authors make these observations about Darby:

> What separated Darby's dispensationalism was his novel method of biblical interpretation, which consisted of a strict literalism, the absolute separation of Israel and the church into two distinct peoples of God, and the separation of the rapture (the "catching away" of the church) from Christ's Second Coming. At the rapture, he said, Christ will come for his saints; and at the Second Coming, he will come with his saints.[43]

Darby (1800-1882) began his ministry as a curate in the Church of Ireland. He had an evangelistic zeal and persuaded many Roman Catholics in his parish to place their full trust in Christ alone, apart from the church.

Due to some politics in the day with the Archbishop of Dublin and King George IV, Darby resigned in protest. Not long after, he

---

[43] Mark Galli and Ted Olsen, *131 Christians Everyone Should Know* (Nashville, TN: Broadman & Holman Publishers, 2000), 99–100.

was injured in a horse-riding incident, providing significant down-time that he used to study the Scriptures. Darby would state later that it was during this time that he began to seriously question the commonly-held notion that the Christian church was the fulfillment of the Kingdom prophecies in Isaiah.

Darby was a remarkable man with God-endowed skills. He was involved in Bible translation work from both Hebrew and Greek into several languages. His Darby study Bible was translated into French, German, and English. (His linguistic skills were well-known, though he declined to participate in the revision work of the King James Bible led by two British scholars, Westcott and Hort).[44] Darby wrote poetry and hymns, he created 32-volumes of Bible commentaries, and translated scholarly works into German, French, and English.

As Darby's theology matured with reflection and time, the three non-negotiables of Dispensationalism (as noted by Ryrie and others) became embedded in his works. He saw a distinction between Israel and the church which affected his eschatology (his view on last things, end-times).

While many of his day were premillennial, no known Bible commentator would have been pre-tribulational concerning the Rapture of the Church. Darby's eschatology grew out of his hermeneutic.[45] He was committed to studying the Bible in its historical and grammatical context. Darby's views on eschatology greatly influenced American dispensationalists – though his

---

[44]https://www.stempublishing.com/authors/darby/MISCELLA/330 11E.html. He was a critic of both the KJV and RV.

[45] This deals with the art and science of biblical interpretation.

ecclesiology (view of the church) did not make an impact. Darby was against denominationalism and paid clergy.

Nearly one hundred years before Israel became a nation, Darby predicted this would happen based upon reading the Bible. He wrote the following:

> As far as the world is concerned, Jerusalem is nothing; it is a city trodden down, with neither commerce nor riches nor aught else. Superstition is established there on the sepulchre of the Lord. It is true, indeed, that the kings of the earth are beginning to look that way, because providence is leading in that direction, but as for God, He ever thinks of it; it is always His house, His city. His eyes and His heart are there continually. Now faith understands this.[46]

He would say in another publication that, from God's perspective, "the desolation of the Jewish people...is...but for a moment."[47] Darby was a pioneering spirit in the development of this systematized approach in understanding Scriptures.

With these positive statements, it would be unfair to say that Darby's methodology was accepted by all. The famed "Prince of Preachers," Charles Spurgeon did not appreciate what he felt were novel approaches to the text. While not naming him by name, he indirectly lets the world know he was no fan of Darby:

> Distinctions have been drawn by certain exceedingly wise men (measured by their own estimate of themselves), between the people of God who lived before the coming of Christ, and those who lived afterwards. We have even heard

---

[46] John Nelson Darby, *Studies on the Book of Daniel*, 1848. CW5:151.

[47] Darby, *On 'Days' Signifying 'Years' in Prophetic Language*, 1830. CW2:35.

it asserted that those who lived before the coming of Christ do not belong to the church of God!

We never know what we shall hear next, and perhaps it is a mercy that these absurdities are revealed at one time, in order that we may be able to endure their stupidity without dying of amazement. Why, every child of God in every place stands on the same footing; the Lord has not some children best beloved, some second-rate offspring, and others whom he hardly cares about.

These who saw Christ's day before it came, had a great difference as to what they knew, and perhaps in the same measure a difference as to what they enjoyed while on earth meditating upon Christ; but they were all washed in the same blood, all redeemed with the same ransom price, and made members of the same body.

Israel in the covenant of grace is not natural Israel, but all believers in all ages. Before the first advent, all the types and shadows all pointed one way —they pointed to Christ...Those who lived before Christ were not saved with a different salvation to that which shall come to us. They exercised faith as we must; that faith struggled as ours struggles, and that faith obtained its reward as ours shall.[48]

Granted, that was a lengthy citation! Yet it shows us a historical snapshot of how Darby's views were perceived. Spurgeon, while a tremendous preacher and soulwinner, was not fond of dispensationalism. He rightly understood the differences he had with Darby: he did not see a distinction between the church and Israel – they were both part of the body of Christ.

---

[48] Charles Spurgeon, *Spurgeon's Sermons* Vol 15: 1869 (London), 9.

Spurgeon also capitalized upon a strawman argument that has been made for at least the past one hundred years.[49] Namely, that "Dispensationalism teaches multiple ways of salvation." This caricature has been hard to dismantle - even though no dispensationalist believes that.

Spurgeon wasn't alone with some of the British believers. George Mueller was also against the teachings of Darby (though not in the beginning). Here's his view of Darby's hermeneutics:

> My brother, I am a constant reader of my Bible, and I soon found out that what I was taught to believe (by Darby's Doctrine) did not always agree with what my Bible said. I came to see that I must either part company with John Darby, or my precious Bible, and I chose to cling to my Bible and part from Mr. Darby.[50]

At one time these two great men were striving together in ministry. They had a bitter falling out and it was difficult for friends of both men to watch. The two never reconciled. Part of Mr. Mueller's words here reflect that difficulty.

This is a very quick sketch of Darby's influence. Much more could be stated. However, at a minimum, we can summarize this section by acknowledging the following. It would be *inaccurate* to say either of the following statements:

1) Dispensational concepts originated with Darby, and
2) Today's dispensationalism is identical to Darby's teachings.

---

[49] Thankfully, some non-dispensationalists are recognizing this historical error and are no longer repeating this serious allegation.

[50] Jonas Alexis, *Christianity and Rabbinic Judaism: A History of Conflict* Vol 2. (Bloomington, IN: Westbow Press, 2013), 200.

To the first statement, we have noted already that dispensational thoughts can be found in many of the ancient writings. As to the second thought, dispensationalism has seen revisions and modifications in its history. Those who have claimed the title of "Dispensationalists" have continually subjected their beliefs to the authority of Scripture – and adjusted as Scripture necessitated it.

American Dispensationalism

While it is true Darby casts a shadow over dispensationalism (as a system), his American counterparts gave dispensationalism a different flavor. Darby was strongly against denominationalism and his views of ecclesiology had little impact upon American dispensationalists.[51] Darby believed the church was in ruins and needed a fresh start.[52] Further, he felt that 2 Timothy 3 predicted the destruction of the church of his day. Americans held to the truth that not even the gates of Hell could stop God's church.

Thomas Ice has written a helpful article on the development of Dispensational thought prior to Darby.[53] He underscores rudimentary dispensational schemes in Justin Martyr (110-165), Irenaeus (130-200), Tertullian (160-220), Methodius (d. 311), and Victorinus of Petau (d. 304).

---

[51] The schism with Darby and Mueller is traced back to Darby's view on the church.

[52] Christianity Today. https://www.christianitytoday.com/history/people/pastorsandpreachers/john-nelson-darby.html.

[53] Thomas D. Ice, "A Short History of Dispensationalism," *Article Archives* (2009): 37.

In this same article, Ice sketches a brief history of dispensational development in America. James Brookes and Adoniram Judson Gordon (for whom Gordon College and Gordon-Conwell Seminary are named) were the early pioneers in the States. It was Gordon who actually led the famous evangelist D.L. Moody to embrace a dispensational scheme for biblical interpretation.

Other contributors to the American-flavored dispensationalism would have included A.C. Gaebelein, William Blackstone, and C.I. Scofield (most remembered for his reference study Bible). These men would have taught their eschatology in Prophetic Conferences such as Niagara Bible Conference and Winona Lake.

L.S. Chafer was influential in establishing Dallas Seminary as a bastion of dispensationalism. His teachings helped the next generation of dispensational leaders including John Walvoord, Harry Ironside, Henry Thiessen, Dwight Pentecost, J. Vernon McGee, Norman Geisler, and Charles Ryrie. Hal Lindsey, author of many books including *The Late, Great Planet Earth*, was also a Dallas graduate and a believer in the principles of dispensationalism.

Perhaps one of the strongest voices in American dispensationalism has been Charles Ryrie. He has written scores of articles and multiple books. Some would say, "He wrote *the* book on dispensationalism." The three non-negotiables were articulated by him. If you haven't read his book, I'd definitely recommend it.

After you read the book in your hands, and then tackle Ryrie's, you will find that there's still a wealth of information to absorb. Renald Showers (*There Really is a Difference*) has made some valuable contributions. Others would include Michael Vlach and Ron Bigalke. Mike Stallard and the Council on Dispensational Hermeneutics gets you into the finer points of dispensational theology.

American dispensationalists like to vote for politicians that are pro-Israel.[54] Why? Does that even matter? Due to a literal reading of Genesis 12 (the Abrahamic Covenant), dispensationalists have taught the importance of being a friend to Israel, the physical descendants of Abraham. In America, we have tried to continually appoint leaders who understood the promise of blessing to those who befriend Israel. We want the blessing God promises to those who bless Israel.

Dispensationalists have stressed the distinction that today's Church is not spiritual Israel. Because of this distinction, the groundwork is placed for a pre-tribulational view of the Rapture. Dispensationalists view the tribulation as the time of "Jacob's trouble" (Jeremiah 30.7) and not the time of the "Church's trouble!" Much of this was articulated in the early American Bible / Prophetic Conferences.

So, despite Darby being dubbed the "Father of Dispensationalism," the direction here in the States has taken a different path. These differences are primarily found in the areas of denominationalism.

---

[54] Jonathan Merritt, "Understanding the Evangelical Obsession with Israel," *America: The Jesuit Review* (December, 2017). https://www.americamagazine.org/politics-society/2017/12/11/understanding-evangelical-obsession-israel.

History of Dispensationalism

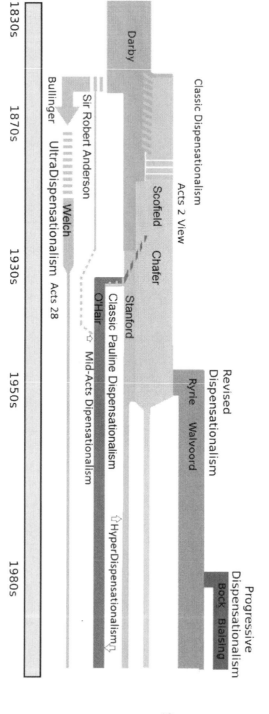

So what?

If you're the type of person that hates history, this chapter has been difficult – no matter its brevity! If a system should be tried by its fidelity to Scriptures, why bother with any historical overview? That's a fair question and I'm not sure there's one definitive answer.

There are a few reasons why I would devote time to providing some background material. First, anyone who claims to be a dispensationalist should understand how God moved in history to keep a commitment to a historical-grammatical hermeneutic alive.

Secondly, it's good for dispensationalists to acknowledge that Darby wasn't perfect and that his view of denominationalism was rejected by American dispensationalists.

Finally, if we fail to learn from history, we're bound to keep making the same mistakes over and over again.

This has been a very brief overview detailing the "Father of Dispensationalism's" impact as well as noting some of the major players in American dispensationalism. At a minimum, here's what I hope you would at least consider from this section:

1. Dispensationalism isn't an invented doctrine from the 1800s.
2. Dispensationalism isn't the position of ignorant, uneducated people.
3. Dispensationalism anticipated the return of Israel to her land.
4. Dispensationalism teaches that God has a future plan for Israel.
5. Dispensationalism consistently interprets Scripture based upon its historical and grammatical context.
6. Dispensationalism interprets prophecy literally rather than spiritually.

Dispensationalism provides answers for today's problems. The postmillennial doctrine that the world would get better as the church ushered in the Kingdom fell out of popularity with the world wars. Dispensationalism offered believers the ultimate hope - that Jesus could come at any moment.

Summary

The key take-aways to remember from this chapter are:

1. Dispensational and covenant theologies are *both* relatively recent inventions as full-blown theological systems.
2. Both systems find hints and seed thoughts from early church history that matures into their respective systems.
3. While John Darby is an important character, dispensationalism doesn't live or die with him. He had his strengths and his flaws - just like all of us.
4. The most important validator for any system is its faithfulness to the biblical text.
5. American dispensationalism does not share Darby's ecclesiology.
6. Dispensationalism believes that God has not cast off [physical] Israel forever.

Chapter 3

THE DISPENSATIONS

How has God governed His "House"

"The Bible is God's declaratory revelation to man containing the great truths about God, about man, about history, about salvation, and about prophecy that God wanted us to know." – John F. Walvoord[55]

Chapter Aims

1. Attain a basic understanding of key differences between Dispensationalism and Covenant Theology.
2. Identify the components that signal a dispensational change
3. List the seven dispensations typically associated with Scofield's teaching.

Introduction

Up to this point, we've used some broad strokes to set the stage for the next several chapters. What have we learned so far? In our first chapter, we covered many important terms that are part of any

---

[55] John F. Walvoord, "Why I Believe the Bible." https://walvoord.com/article/316

hermeneutical conversation. We defined not only a *dispensation*, but also, we defined *dispensationalism* and the basics of this system. Remember this definition?

> Dispensationalism is a system of historical progression consisting of a series of stages in God's self-revelation to man, anchored by a historical-grammatical hermeneutic which results in a distinction between Israel and the Church and which also unifies progressive revelation around a doxological purpose.

Many of the key terms associated with this system are now familiar. These terms include words like *hermeneutics, eschatology, oikonomia,* and others. As we begin to compare dispensationalism to covenant theology in the next few chapters, it will become apparent that there is a noticeable difference between the two systems.

For now, here are a few thoughts to help us keep dispensationalism and covenant theology separate in our minds. These two systems are recognized as the most popular hermeneutical systems used today.

Dispensationalism and Covenant Theology are recognized as the most popular hermeneutical systems today.

Covenant theology uses the concept of a *theological covenant(s)* as its organizing principle for theology, hermeneutics, and an understanding of redemptive history.

The implications of this principle are that there is much continuity between the testaments, the church is part of the same people as Israel, and the Rapture is not pre-tribulational.

The organizing principle(s) used by dispensationalists is that of stewardship to the progressive revelation that has been delivered. The implications of this are that there is more discontinuity between the testaments, the church is distinctly different from the nation of Israel, and the Rapture will occur before the Tribulation begins. Obviously, there is much more to these two systems, but this is enough to show that significant differences exist.

	Organizing Principles	Church & Israel	Rapture	Priority of Testament
DT[56]	*Stewarding Revelation Delivered*	*Two Distinct People*	*Before Tribulation*	*OT with emphasis on progressive revelation*
CT	*Theological Covenants Implied*	*One People*	*After Tribulation*	*NT with emphasis on cumulative revelation*

Contrasting Dispensational and Covenant Theology

So, where do we go from here? We know dispensationalism is a system, it has three non-negotiables, and is very different from covenant theology. Great. But what else should we know? In this section, we take a look at dispensationalism as a system and how it understands the biblical record.

In this chapter, we will answer the following questions: 1) How do you identify a dispensational change in the text? 2) Does the Bible itself validate these dispensational changes? 3) What are the typical dispensational divisions found within dispensationalism?

---

[56] DT = Dispensational Theology; CT = Covenant Theology

Identifying Dispensational Changes

Consider just about any family in just about any place! They all go through stages. You've gone through stages as well. Remember your original diet? Breakfast? That was milk. Lunch? Oh, that was milk also. Dinner? Snacks? In-between feedings? Yep, always milk. I would hope in your current stage, your parents allow you to have something else!

Do you remember going to kindergarten? Junior high? High school? College? Do you remember getting your license? These are stages – shifts in the way your life is governed. Perhaps marriage is ahead for you. Then, perhaps, come the children. One day, the kids are out of the house, and grandkids come to visit. Each of these stages requires a different parenting / governing exercise.[57]

In God's household, He has governed differently at stages of history as well. These variations, these changes in "parenting" His world, will help us identify these dispensational shifts. The concepts are similar to our houses in which we were raised.

We know, almost intuitively, that as we read the Bible, things have changed. In the Old Testament, they all gathered in Jerusalem in the one temple. In the gospels, they had the rebuilt temple as well as synagogues. Today, we have churches (and in some parts of the US - they're on every corner!) We have a pastor, not a priest. All believers can function as a believer-priest, not just those from the tribe of Levi. No one brings turtle doves or lambs to church for a sacrifice. From a dispensational point of view, these are all evidences of a dispensational change.

---

[57] Do you remember our steward, the oikonomos? He is involved in these different stages and his master sets different expectations for his soon-to-be adult son as opposed to that same son when he was three years old. It's the same child – but at a different stage requiring different governing techniques.

What should Bible students be looking for to know *when* there is a dispensational change? Are these dispensations "biblical" or do dispensationalists bring their preconceived ideas to the text? In hermeneutical terms, is the concept of a dispensation *exegetical* (meaning, it comes *from the text*) or *eisegetical* (meaning, it is brought *to the text*)? Clearly, these are important questions to consider!

Covenant theologians read the Bible through the lens of theological covenants. From a dispensational point of view, these are extra-biblical (as they are not in the text).[58] Thus, when something extra-biblical becomes the lens through which Scripture is read, dispensationalists see this as bringing one's preconceived ideas *to the text* rather than pulling the meaning *from the text*. Yet, are dispensationalists guilty of doing the same?

Cyrus I. Scofield

In the Scofield Reference Bible, C.I. Scofield made the dispensational system popular. It wasn't uncommon for me to hear preachers as I was growing up say something like, "Turn in your Scofield Bible to page…" Yet, unknown to many, he had additional writings as well. In one of his works he said,

> The Scriptures divide time, by which is meant the entire period from the creation of Adam to the "new heaven and a new earth" of Rev. 21:1, into seven unequal periods, called, usually, "dispensations" (Eph. 3:2), although these periods are also called "ages" (Eph. 2:7) and "days"—as, "day of the Lord," etc.[59]

---

[58] I have used *extra-biblical* intentionally. This term isn't synonymous with *non-biblical*. It may be (and granted, in this context I believe that it is); but it doesn't have to be.

[59] C. I. Scofield, *Rightly Dividing the Word of Truth (2 Tim. 2:15):*

Note his starting point: "The *Scriptures* divide time..." As a brief digression, the thrust of dispensationalism isn't about how we divide time (that's only a small portion). The bigger picture is what responsibility – what stewardship – was *dispensed* to man during that time. While there is a time element, it should be secondary to the actual stewarding responsibility that has been committed.

The terminology Scofield used to describe these seven dispensations were as follows:

1. Man innocent
2. Man under conscience
3. Man in authority over the earth (later, Civil | Human Government)
4. Man under promise (or, Patriarchal Rule)
5. Man under law
6. Man under grace (or, under the Spirit - church age)
7. Man under the personal reign of Christ (Millennial Kingdom)

Charles Ryrie

Ryrie produced the following chart in his book *Dispensationalism* to illustrate his understanding of the dispensational shifts that occurred in Scripture.[60]

Ten Outline Studies of the More Important Divisions of Scripture (Philadelphia: Philadelphia School of the Bible, 1921), 20.

[60] Ryrie, *Dispensationalism*, 54.

THE DISPENSATIONS

Name	Scripture	Responsibilities	Judgment(s)
Innocency	Genesis 1:3-3:6	Keep Garden Do not eat one fruit Fill, subdue earth Fellowship with God	Curses, and physical and spiritual death
Conscience	Genesis 3:7-8:14	Do good	Flood
Civil Government	Genesis 8:15-11:9	Fill earth Capital punishment	Forced scattering by confusion of languages
Patriarchal Rule	Genesis 11:10-Exodus 18:27	Stay in Promised Land Believe and obey God	Egyptian bondage and wilderness wanderings
Mosaic Law	Exodus 19:1-John 14:30	Keep the law Walk with God	Captivities
Grace	Acts 2:1-Revelation 19:21	Believe on Christ Walk with Christ	Death Loss of rewards
Millennium	Revelation 20:1-15	Believe and obey Christ and His government	Death Great White Throne Judgment

Dispensationalists recognize that some of these dispensations are implied rather than explicit. Because of this admission, no dispensationalist has made the number of dispensations a non-negotiable. Many like the number "seven" – whether that is logical deduction or a fancy with the "perfect" number. Nevertheless, if one held to only five dispensations, he could still be a "dispensationalist."

Just as dispensationalists believe in "covenants," it is not strange to find covenant theologians who believe in "dispensations." Indeed, since it is a biblical word, we would be shocked if they did not. As stated, the non-negotiables concern one's hermeneutic (normal, historical, grammatical), a recognition of two peoples (church and Israel), and an understanding of God's doxological purpose. Nowhere is it stated, "A belief in dispensations!"

Dispensations explicit in the Scriptures

What dispensations are explicitly mentioned in Scripture and what are implied because of noticing dispensational changes? First, all should agree that *there is a future kingdom* (though not all believe

77

in a literal millennium, or a 1000-year reign). In 2 Samuel 7, the Davidic Covenant promises a future seed - a "son of David" - will rule from David's throne. This is also the basis of Revelation 20. If you take the Scriptures at face value, then we must admit that Jesus is not ruling in Jerusalem from David's throne *at this moment*.

Secondly, all should agree that *there was a period where God ruled man by the law*. This is given in Exodus and repeated in Deuteronomy. The prophets call out the people for disobeying the law. John 1.17 says that the "law was given by Moses," and that grace and truth were the work of Jesus Christ. Paul, writing to the Romans, does much to remind the believer that he is not "under the law" but under grace.

Thirdly, as contrasted with law, *there is now a new governing principle God has for His people*. Scofield referred to it as grace - yet, most dispensationalists understand that this word does raise some objections. At first glance, it may seem to imply that there was "no grace" until Jesus came. Yet, Noah "found grace in the eyes of the Lord." While *grace* is a biblical word (as in the contrast provided in Romans), it doesn't fully articulate the dispensational change.

Perhaps another way to look at the shift that occurs after the law is rendered inoperative is to see the ministry of the Holy Spirit. In the Old Testament, He is there, but often in the background. But on the day of Pentecost, that changes.

From Pentecost (Acts 2) and onward, He seals, fills, and indwells believers *permanently*. He baptizes believers into the body of Christ according to 1 Corinthians 12.13. We do not live under the law, but we "walk in the Spirit" (Galatians 5). Thus, it is fairly easy to observe the changes in the way God governs man (through the law, through His indwelling Spirit, and by personally reigning on earth during the kingdom).

These three dispensations are understood as being explicitly stated in Scripture. Personally, I believe a fourth dispensation is explicit as well. According to Galatians 3, *Paul contrasts law with a promise* given 430 years previously.

His argument is to show that the dispensational shift to being governed by the law did not void out future blessings that were given by the promise (to Abraham). Paul highlights a shift in God's dealing with mankind and refers to a previous period as "promise" (the name followed by Scofield and since it refers to Abraham, others have called it the patriarchal rule).

Dispensations implicit in the Scripture

The dispensations of *innocence* (Genesis 1), *conscience* (Genesis 3), and human *government* (Genesis 9) are not as explicitly stated. One can see them, but there is no express statement in Scripture that shows the transitions between them.

Understanding why dispensationalists normally hold to these three dispensations – even without explicit Scriptural statements – brings us to the issue of how to determine dispensational changes.

Dispensationalists study the Scriptures, looking for primary and secondary characteristics of dispensations. These characteristics allow one to recognize when God is beginning to deal with His creation – His house (*oikos*) – in a different manner.

Primary Characteristics

According to Ryrie (and others), three primary characteristics can be identified as markers to a new dispensation beginning (or, a previous one coming to an end).

First, we look for a *change in God's governing relationship* with mankind. Secondly, we look for a *change in man's responsibility*. Finally, we look to see if there is a development or progression, a *change in God's revelation* that introduces these transitions.[61] Let's consider each of these individually.

New governing relationship.

In the Garden, when it was just Adam and Eve, mankind had a perfect theocracy. God personally ruled over His creation and met with Adam (and Eve) each day. His rule was personal, regular, and intimate. When Adam and Eve lost their innocence, this dynamic changed. Note that all Bible readers recognize that after Adam's fall, those meetings "in the cool of the day" in paradise ended.

Upon the fall of man, with guilt and sin now ever-present, God would no longer meet with Adam daily as He once did. God would now exert His rule over His creation *indirectly*. His law, written upon man's heart, would speak. Today, we refer to this "inner voice" of right and wrong as man's conscience. The word *conscience* literally means "with (*con*) knowledge (*science*)". Human beings are now born "with knowledge" – a conscience.

After the flood incident, God allowed man to rule himself in clans, tribes, and eventually kingdoms. Human government was created. For the first time, God had delegated to man the authority to put people to death. This is quite different from Adam and Eve living with their family after the Fall. When Cain put Abel to death, there was a huge price for taking a life. This was a change.

The governmental system had an epic failure at the Tower of Babel. God intended for them to scatter; they chose to unite. God intended for them to be His representatives across the globe; they built a pagan altar at Babel instead. God devised another way to

---

[61] Charles Ryrie, *Dispensationalism*, 34. (It's the application of both primary and secondary characteristics that allow dispensationalists to recognize different dispensational shifts in Genesis 1, 3, and 9.

cause them to scatter – He confused their languages and ability to communicate as "one people united."

God then chose to govern the world through a representative family (Abram) and He offered them the hope of a future promise. Yet, mankind had trouble holding onto this hope. So, God gave, through Moses, His covenant of law for His people to follow. This law contained 619 ordinances and covered nearly every detail of private and public life. This covenant, from a Jewish perspective, wasn't a list of do's and don'ts. Rather, it was the binding agreement for a relationship (the emphasis was *relationship* and not *rules*).[62]

The law was designed to show man's flaws, shortcomings, and sin. It was meant to be a tutor, a schoolmaster to point to an even greater truth. Thus, God brought about a new administration (a new economy or dispensation) of governing His people - through His indwelling Spirit.

Ultimately, this progression ends where it all started. God will personally, regularly, and intimately rule over His creation on earth. He will sit upon the throne of David, in Jerusalem, and finally bring about world peace. Ultimately, His kingdom and government will have no end. Where paradise had been lost, it will finally be restored. God will make all things new.

This progression, this change of administration doesn't mean that God couldn't settle on a governing style and kept trying until

---

[62] A strong argument could be made that the Covenant at Sinai was where God became the Husband and took Israel as His wife. From this point on, anytime she follows the pagan gods of Canaan, the picture is that of playing the harlot, of going "whoring" after other gods. In effect, from the point of this relational covenant and onward, unfaithfulness to the terms of the covenant are treated as [spiritual] adultery.

He found one that He liked! Rooted in the concept of *oikonomia* is the rule of a house.[63]

I have five children - two are married, and three are in school. My oldest isn't governed like my youngest - she doesn't even live in my house. She has advanced beyond that stage. I don't set her bedtime. I don't remind her to brush her teeth. In effect, I don't treat her "like a child." In a sense, she'll always be my "child" but my parenting relationship with her advances through different stages over time.

Change in man's responsibility.

As God's *oikos* (the relationship in His house) has matured, so have the responsibilities. We can understand this as we think about our relationship with our parents and with our children. Changes take place for which we must be responsible. As a full-grown, married man, my relationship to my own parents looks differently than when I was a ten-year old. In like manner, as the firstborn, my responsibilities have changed in regards to this relationship as well.

Under the administration of innocence, man's responsibilities were much simpler. Adam was responsible to keep the Garden. Additionally, he was responsible to obey God's command regarding the fruit from the Tree of Knowledge of Good and Evil.

When Adam and Eve lost their innocence, their conscience was awakened. Their living quarters had changed along with the way God previously had met with them. In essence, their responsibility was to obey the dictates of their conscience.

After the flood, mankind found himself once again in a different administration. He was now responsible to fill the earth. He was responsible to obey the laws of the land (government). He

---

[63] Oikos (house) + nomos (law)…it is the rule of a house…

had also been entrusted with the responsibility of carrying out capital punishment.

As man spread out after the Babel incident, those who followed Jehovah were responsible to stay in the promised land and obey God. Eventually, they left the land and went to Egypt - a decision that affected their tribes for over 400 years. Those who were once free became enslaved until God sent a deliverer, Moses.

As the nation was brought back to the land, man was now responsible to abide by the covenant that had been made. Due to an understanding of progressive relationship, we observe that Jacob and his sons were not responsible to abide by this covenant before the Egyptian captivity. This change in government through means of a covenant was something new. The covenant is sometimes referred to as "the law," the "law of Moses," or the "Mosaic Covenant."

When Jesus came to the earth, He fulfilled the law and man was now responsible to believe in Him and to walk in the Spirit. Nowhere, under the Old Covenant, had man ever been instructed to walk in the Spirit. This was a new responsibility. In effect, it was a dispensational change.

In the final dispensation, the kingdom, man is responsible to obey the King who is physically reigning over them. While there is a sense in which the phrase "kingdom" can refer to God's spiritual rule over all His house - the prophecies in the Old and New Testaments point to something greater - He will physically return, set up His kingdom, and rule from Jerusalem upon David's throne.

Advanced (New) Revelation.

Within each dispensational shift we find God providing advanced revelation that brought about a change in man's responsibilities. Do you realize that Abraham never read a single passage in his "Bible?" Neither did Noah or Adam! Revelation was given progressively as God's "house" entered different economies or administrations of God's rule.

During the time of Innocence, revelation was relatively light. Presumably, God told Adam about creation - but concerning His plan of redemption, nothing was said (or, technically, nothing is ever *recorded* biblically to say that it was). It would have been *irrelevant* during the dispensation of innocence.

Yet, when the dispensation shifted, God provided additional information (revelation). Immediately, He spoke of a coming redeemer, the "seed of the woman" who would come (Genesis 3.15). As man followed his conscience, he also knew God had a way to recreate paradise once again. Obviously, they saw "through a glass darkly," but they had been given hope through God's revelation.

Throughout the Old Testament, God gave more light that brought the picture into a little bit more focus. But, with the preaching of John the Baptist, the shadows became substance. Jesus, the God-man, was here on the earth offering the kingdom that had been promised.

During the time after the flood, God instituted human government. God provided revelation concerning capital punishment. Until Genesis 9, *all* death by the hands of another was a violation of one's conscience. Now, God was instructing mankind that there were times when the right thing to do was to put a person to death. God instructed man to establish these governments and fill the earth. They did not and instead they decided to gather and build a tower to heaven.

After the time of Babel, God revealed an enhancement of His promise in Genesis 3.15. He was choosing one man - and his descendants - from out of all the earth to bring this promised redeemer. He chose Abraham and told him how his seed would be great. He laid out the boundaries for a land that would be for his descendants forever.

Of course, the entire Mosaic covenant was new revelation. Paul makes this clear that until the law, death reigned. Yet, sin is not imputed where there is no law (Romans 5). Once law was given - once additional revelation was provided - then man's responsibilities (and his accountability to God) were greater.

When Jesus came, He was *the* revelation from God. No one would have understood that He would fulfill the law, and then place His righteousness on the account of those who believed in Him. This was revelation that was revolutionary.

So, when dispensationalists are looking for a change from one dispensation to the next, they look for three primary factors: 1) Is there a change in the way God *rules* over His people? 2) Is there a change in additional *revelation* God provides for His people? (The question is not, "Is there more *illumination* given?" Specifically, we are looking for new revelation.) Finally, 3) Is there a change in man's *responsibilities* before God?

Dispensation	Governing Relation	Man's Responsibility	New Revelation
Innocence	*Theocracy*	*Keep the Garden; Obey*	*Everything was new*
Conscience	*Indirect, internal law*	*Obey dictates of conscience*	*Coming Redemption*
Government	*Man ruled himself*	*Fill up the earth*	*Capital Punishment*
Promise	*Representative government*	*Stay in Promised Land; obey God*	*Abrahamic Covenant*
Law	*Binding Covenant*	*Abide by Covenant*	*The Mosaic Law*
Spirit	*Indwelling Spirit*	*Walk in the Spirit*	*Christian living*
Kingdom	*Personal rule*	*Obey the King*	*Faith becomes sight*

Understanding the Primary Characteristics

85

Secondary Characteristics

Jerald Finney, in his book *God Betrayed*, mentions three secondary characteristics that dispensationalists also look for to determine if there has been a dispensational shift. These secondary elements are not unique to Finney and many Bible students find that these secondary elements are helpful.

First, God applies a "test" of obedience to see if man will obey or disobey. Secondly, mankind inevitably has a "failure" to that test. Finally, this brings about judgment upon mankind.[64] The testing is in regards to the responsibility and is virtually synonymous.

When we say God "tests" man - we don't intend to paint a picture of the Great Tinkerer Upstairs who is looking for a way that will work! God is omniscient, knowing the beginning from the ending. As Ryrie notes,

> Opponents of dispensationalism, who insist that such testing on God's part makes Him little more than an experimenter apparently not knowing how things will turn out, in reality fail to understand the purpose of testing in general. After all, a dispensational test is no different essentially from the tests spoken of by James in chapter 1 of his epistle. Such tests are not for the purpose of enlightening God but for the purpose of bringing out what is in people, whether faith or failure.[65]

Considering that tests are part of man's lot, the concept of rooting this into dispensationalism (test, failure, judgment) doesn't seem to be far-fetched at all. Let's notice how this works.

---

[64] Jerald Finney, *God Betrayed: Separation of Church and State: The Biblical Principles and the American Application* (Austin, TX: Kerygma Publishing, 2008), 138.

[65] Ryrie, *Dispensationalism*, 34.

In the dispensation of innocence, man's test is the tree. Will they eat that fruit and disobey, or will they remain obedient to what they know to do? Adam and Eve failed the test. The judgment is seen in their eviction from the Garden (along with the other aspects mentioned in Genesis 3).

In the dispensation of conscience, the test is simple: Will man follow the dictates of his conscience? He failed. In Genesis 6, the thoughts of man's heart were only evil continually. How did God judge? He sent a flood.

In the dispensation of government, man was to spread out and rule as God's Image-Bearer. What did man do? He gathered everyone together to build a tower, a place of pagan worship, at Babel. How did God judge? He confounded their languages.

In the dispensation of promise, when God was ruling through His patriarchal representatives, they were to inherit the land. What did they do? They found themselves in Egypt - not to simply get bread. They called it home. How did God judge? They were enslaved to the Egyptians until He sent His deliverer, Moses.

During the dispensation of law, the longest period in the Old Testament, the children of Israel were to obey God's covenant law. They failed. And the judgments were multiplied. The Northern Kingdom was taken into Assyria. The Southern Captivity was taken to Babylon. Ultimately, Jerusalem was destroyed (70AD) with that nation being temporarily disinherited from its land.

During the dispensation of the Spirit's rule in our lives, New Testament Church saints are tested with our obedience to the Great Commission. Mankind, as a whole, is tested to believe this Gospel and accept Christ. God will judge at the end of this dispensation through the Tribulation period of seven years.

In the final dispensation, Christ will set up His physical kingdom and the world will have one test: Will they obey Him? We know He will rule with a rod of iron and that some will rebel. The judgment for those? The Great White Throne Judgment and an eternity in a Lake of Fire.

Granted, that's a good amount of information to try to process and digest. As previously provided for the primary characteristics, here is a chart notating how the secondary characteristics work in dispensationalism. Notice how the "test" and the "responsibility" are virtually synonymous in this chart.

Dispensation	Test	Judgment
Innocence	Don't eat the tree!	Eviction from Garden
Conscience	Obey conscience	The Flood
Government	Spread out and rule	Confusion of languages
Promise	Stay in the land	Egyptian Bondage
Law	Obey God's law	Exiled from land, destruction of temple
Spirit	Obey Great Commission	Tribulation
Kingdom	Obey Christ	Great White Throne Judgment; Eternal Banishment from Kingdom

Understanding the Secondary Characteristics

The biblical record

How do these primary and secondary characteristics have any bearing on how we understand the biblical record? The unifying theme that is running behind the scenes here is the concept of *progressive revelation*. From a covenant theological perspective, the emphasis is on *cumulative revelation* – both of these concepts cause the Bible to be read and understood differently.

Cumulative revelation starts at Genesis 1 and already knows how the story ends in Revelation. Thus, in reading through the narrative, there is a *conscious* effort to read New Testament truths into the Old Testament narrative. The emphasis here is on continuity.

Progressive revelation emphasizes discontinuity. It begins in Genesis 1 and reads the narrative from the perspective of the original audience, who didn't know how it all ended up. Because of this, notice two samplings of how salvation was understood in the Old Testament saints:

> This article aims to remove this confusion and to establish that Old Testament saints were saved by grace alone, *through faith in Christ alone.* Old Testament saints were saved in the same way as New Testament saints.[66]

> This dispensationalist's answer to the question of the relation of grace and law is this: The basis of salvation in every age is the death of Christ; the requirement for salvation in every age is faith; the object of faith in every age is God; the content of faith changes in the various dispensations.[67]

These two statements are irreconcilable. The first statement, from a covenant theological position, states that all Old Testament saints were saved through faith *in Christ.* The dispensationalist counters, "Yes, they were saved *by faith* - but not necessarily *in Christ.* After all, His name was unknown."

---

[66] David Murray, "Our View of the Old Testament." *Puritan Reformed Journal* 02:2 (July 2010): 5. [Emphasis added.]

[67] Ryrie, *Dispensationalism.* 115.

Ryrie, speaking for the dispensationalist, is adamant (as so many other dispensationalists have been) that salvation is grounded in the substitutionary atonement of Christ. His death is what makes salvation possible in any dispensation. This salvation, rooted in Christ's death, is always by grace and through *faith* – always. Dispensationalism has never taught multiple ways of salvation.

The problem with the two statements, representing opposing views, is that Murray dogmatically states that Old Testament saints

> *No OT saint was saved by faith in Christ alone, but all OT saints were saved by grace through faith.*

were saved *through faith in Christ alone*. This is a statement that is easily disproven. In fact, dispensationalists are even more dogmatic: "No OT Saint was saved by placing faith in Christ alone, but all OT saints were saved by grace through faith."

Consider Genesis 15.6 and the imputation of righteousness to Abraham. Did it come by *faith in Christ alone*? No. Rather, it came because Abraham believed (had faith) what God had said (that is, God's Word – His revelation during that period of progressive revelation) about his numerous descendants. Abraham was not looking for "Jesus Christ to come, be born of a virgin, and die on a cross for his sins…"

Consider Abraham – he's the father of all that believe! He is a perfect Old Testament test-case. How was he saved? Or, better, what was the cause of him receiving God's imputed righteousness. There's no surprise, for the Bible answers this in Genesis 15.6. Abraham believed God's word concerning the abundance of his seed and this was counted to him for righteousness.

This isn't meant to imply that no knowledge of the coming Messiah was available to OT saints. But, it would be hard-pressed to read Genesis 3.15 and say, "Adam looked for God to come in the flesh, to become God's anointed (Messiah/ Christ) and die on a Roman cross for the payment for all our sins." But, he most definitely had faith *in God's Word*. Don't we read that "Faith comes by hearing, and hearing by the word of God..."?

This comes back to Ryrie's dispensational answer. Salvation has always been by faith. From God's perspective, salvation is grounded in the finished work of Christ. From man's perspective, the object of that faith was *in the Word* that God had revealed up to that time.

Remember, God, who is outside of time, is able to say about the redemptive work of Jesus: "the Lamb slain before the foundation of the world," (Revelation 13.8). God knew His plan of salvation and what it would take. Again, this is how He could remind Abraham that God would provide *Himself* a lamb... (Genesis 22.8).

In this discussion of how to read the Scriptures, it really is a question of testament priority. Do we read the Bible *forward* or *backward*? When I read Psalm 22, is that David prophesying what Christ would say at Calvary? Or, is that the words of David, personally, in a great trial that the future Son of David took and applied to His great suffering?

A dispensationalist starts in the historical context and interprets David's words based on his revelation, his knowledge, his circumstances. Then, it connects David's situation to the Son of David's crucifixion.

The cumulative revelation approach to Psalm 22 is different. Why? Neither position starts at the same point; thus, they end up in different areas. The cumulative approach reads Psalm 22, and already knows Jesus quotes it. The preaching of Psalm 22 becomes entirely Christocentric. This isn't a bad thing - but it overlooks an important detail. Before these were the words of God incarnate - they were the words of a human believer. David's emotion, when understood in that light, becomes a great comfort when we feel abandoned or forsaken. We know we are not the first to feel that way. Further, we know theologically that God never leaves us.

McCune reminds us that "[p]rogressive revelation emphasizes the movement of history toward a goal, which Scripture describes as the "fullness of times" (Eph 1:10), a period dispensationalists call the *millennial kingdom*.[68]" Before we judge an Old Testament saint by New Testament standards, let's make sure we understand how much knowledge had been given to them.

The Bible didn't float down from heaven as a completed masterpiece. It was over 1600 years in the making. It involved three languages, multiple continents and an acknowledgement that many of its writers never knew each other.

One more example about understanding this progressive revelation should suffice. Dispensationalists are almost always pre-tribulational when it comes to the Rapture. Covenant theologians rarely are. Once I heard a covenant preacher use 1 Corinthians 15 to prove the Rapture was post-tribulational (or at least, pre-wrath of God). He mentioned that *Paul* said this would occur at the last trump. Then he took his

The Bible didn't float down from heaven as a completed masterpiece – it was 1600 years in the making.

---

[68] Rolland McCune, *A Systematic Theology of Biblical Christianity: Prolegomena and the Doctrines of Scripture, God, and Angels*, vol. 1 (Allen Park, MI: Detroit Baptist Theological Seminary, 2009), 108.

audience to Revelation where *John* talked about the Seven Trumpets.

His argument, on the surface, was convincing. Except, there was one problem. No one in the 60's reading 1 Corinthians could have cross-referenced a book that would not be written for another twenty-five years. In other words, no one at First Christian Church of Corinth read Paul's letter and flipped over to Revelation and said, "Aha! - Now we know what he meant!"

Paul's meaning needs to be grounded in the Corinthian context – the context of the original hearers.

Summary

When the primary characteristics of rule, revelation, and responsibility are considered along with the secondary characteristics of test, failure, and judgment, dispensationalists feel there is warrant to identify the period between the fall of man until the giving of the law with more than one dispensation.

The judgments are upon all of mankind with new revelation and responsibilities being given. It can be shown that man has failed his God-given test and God has changed the way He rules over mankind. With these in mind, the original scheme of seven dispensations will probably remain popular for many years to come.

As we conclude this chapter, you have some interpretative questions to take with you as you read the Bible.

1. How much revelation has been given up to this point in the chronological story of the Bible? (We can't hold OT saints to NT standards - it hasn't been revealed yet...)

2. Has there been a change in the way God is exerting His rule over mankind? Is there a written law or no? Have human governments been instituted yet, or not? Are the believers in

this passage permanently indwelt by the Spirit or are they praying like David, "Take not thy holy spirit from me..." (Psalm 51.10)?

3. Has mankind been given different or additional responsibilities by God?

4. Has there been any world-changing judgments in which nothing remains the same afterwards?

5. Is this prophetic (pointing to the kingdom), historic (looking to the past), or relevant (present-day application)?

Chapter 4

DISPENSATIONAL SHIFTS

Dealing with items that carry-over from
previous dispensations

"The outstanding characteristic of the dispensationalist is the fact that he *believes* every statement of the Bible and gives to it the plain, natural meaning its words imply." Lewis Sperry Chafer[69]

Chapter Aims

1. Articulate why some dispensational elements carry over into a new dispensation, and others do not.
2. Define the biblical concept of a *steward* and his *stewardship*.
3. Understand the implications that come from a *continuous* or *discontinuous* approach to the Scriptures.
4. Explain the concept of "the law of Christ."

---

[69] Lewis Sperry Chafer, *Dispensationalism* (Dallas: Dallas Theological Seminary, 1936), 83.

Introduction

In previous chapters, we have attempted to define our terms and understand a *brief* historical overview of the roots of dispensationalism. Additionally, we have tried to point out how to identify when there is a change in dispensations.

In considering changes within dispensations, does this mean a "clean break," or are there "carryovers" from one to the next? For example, since we are no longer in the dispensation of human government, does that mean we have no responsibility to obey?

In this chapter, we take a look at how dispensational elements sometimes carryover to the next - and sometimes they don't! What's going on with this? Is this an adventure into subjectivity? Or, can we "stand alone on the Word of God" to make these observations?

Oikonomos

We've hinted at this in our definition, the word translated *dispensation* in our Bible is *oikonomia | oikonomos*. These words need to be fleshed out a little to provide some context. As is self-evident, the two words are connected and both are related to a home.

Oikonomia is defined by Spiros Zodhiates as "the position, work, responsibility or arrangement of an administration, as of a house or of property, either one's own or another's (Luke 16:2; Sept.: Is. 22:19)."[70] He also mentions that it is connected to the administrative activity of the owner *or* the steward.

For now, just let that word "steward" stick in your mind. Sometimes we think we know all about stewardship...we'll need to test our presuppositions. Perhaps your church has a month where it

---

[70] Spiros Zodhiates, *The Complete Word Study Dictionary: New Testament* (Chattanooga, TN: AMG Publishers, 2000).

emphasizes stewardship. It may be that your church has a special offering that it connects with a stewardship banquet. Often, in our twenty-first century, the word *stewardship* conjures up ideas pertaining to finances. Is this the complete picture?

Open your Bible for a moment to Luke 16. I'm pulling the text below from the King James Bible. I have substituted an English word for its underlying Greek word. What word is missing?

> And he said also unto his disciples, There was a certain rich man, which had a **oikonomon**; and the same was accused unto him that he had wasted his goods. And he called him, and said unto him, How is it that I hear this of thee? give an account of thy **oikonomias**; for thou mayest be no longer **oikonomein**. Then the **oikonomos** said within himself, What shall I do? for my lord taketh away from me the **oikonomian**: I cannot dig; to beg I am ashamed.[71]

If you said "steward" and "stewardship," you are correct. These related words deal with the steward who has responsibility in the house. This responsibility is his stewardship – it is his dispensation. He is to carry out the administration of the owner.

Stewardship

The job of supervising or taking care of something, such as an organization or property – it's bigger than just finances

Think how this relates to the concept of dispensationalism. The world is God's household; He is the Owner. This means that you and I are the stewards. In God's household, as in any household, the responsibilities change as the children advance in age. Some of

---

[71] Luke 16:1–3.

our childhood responsibilities still stay with us even in adulthood. (As a child, I couldn't wait until I was grown so I wouldn't have to take out the trash...funny thing, adults have trash, too!)

Stewardship

Too often our concept of stewardship is connected to finances. "We're having a Stewardship Banquet!" "Remember as God's stewards to be faithful in tithes and offerings." Note - these are not *incorrect* statements, they are merely *incomplete* statements.

A steward in the New Testament was responsible for the financial affairs of his master's house, but it wasn't limited to financial affairs alone. An Old Testament picture of a steward was Joseph. He had the *authority* and the *responsibility* to rule over Potiphar's house (again, it was not simply overseeing Potiphar's financial investments!) Paul tells us that it is required in stewards that we be found faithful (1 Corinthians 4.2).

Pickering tells us that there are certain implications within the concept of a stewardship as well. First, there is the concept of *time*. "Manage my affairs for this set period of time..." "Take care of this until I return..." While *time* is not essential to the definition of dispensationalism, it is foundational to the concept of stewardship.

Secondly, there is the concept of *testing*. A steward will be watched and he will be held accountable. This is taught in the parables of Christ – especially Luke 16.[72]

I believe we can add a third element to these implications Pickering has set forth. We should also add the concept of *truth*. The steward, in dispensationalism, is held accountable to the truth

---

[72] Ernest Pickering, "Dispensational Theology," *Central Bible Quarterly* 04:1 (Spring 1961): 29-35.

that has been revealed to him. The amount of truth may not be equal, but the accountability to live by the truth revealed remains the same – regardless of which dispensation one is born into.

Three Ingredients for Biblical Stewardship:

1. *Time*
2. *Testing*
3. *Truth*

Dispensational Shifts

Dispensational shifts do not always happen overnight - but they do happen. Transition periods occur as one dispensation ends and another one begins. If someone were to say, "I just don't see any real differences between so-called dispensational shifts…" - perhaps we should simply ask, "Where's your lamb?" The practice of animal sacrifice is not relevant today. Why?

In these transitional moments we see clean breaks from one dispensation to the next. As an example, I don't eat kosher-only food! While visiting Israel years ago, my wife and I were excited near the end of our visit when we found a non-kosher pizzeria! Please pass the bacon, sausage, and pepperoni.

However, not only do we see clean breaks, we also see carryovers - responsibilities from a previous dispensation that are still binding. I still have to submit to human governments (and I get a ticket for speeding even though I'm not "under the law!"). More importantly, the way of salvation shows a carryover, a continuity. Salvation has always been by grace through faith – *always*.

In this section we discuss the clean breaks that are made from dispensation to dispensation as well as understanding what carries over from one to the next. Perhaps of even more relevance, we demonstrate how to know which is which.

It would be inaccurate to say that dispensationalism compartmentalizes all of world history into nice clean boxes! This diversity within how God has administrated His rule doesn't rule out the unifying theme of redemption throughout history.

Graham Scroggie called this the "unfolding drama of redemption."[73] Thus, there is a sense when we discuss the "diversity" of ruling arrangements God made as well as the "unity" in His plan of redemption.

Examples of Carry-Overs and Breaks

Killing was wrong before Exodus 20! Even though it was codified as "law" with the Mosaic Covenant, murder has always been wrong - regardless of the dispensational arrangement. God held Cain accountable for murder under the dispensation of conscience.

If God held Cain accountable, then there was sufficient light for him to know it was wrong - even though the law was over 2000 years away! Additionally, just because we are not "under the law" - we don't have the authority to commit murder "under grace."

How do we identify these continuing principles and why do we think it's ok to eat sausage, pork chops, or honey-baked ham?! Why do we insist certain parts of Leviticus are relevant (be ye holy!) and other parts are not. Leviticus provides a few "abominations" by divine inspiration – and yet, most aren't preached against today. Consider some of the abominable sins found in Leviticus:

1. Homosexuality (Leviticus 18.22)
2. Pork and Shellfish (Leviticus 11.7-10)

---

[73] Graham Scroggie, *The Unfolding Drama of Redemption* (Grand Rapids: Kregel Classics, 1995).

3. Spiritism (Leviticus 19.31)
4. Mixed Fabric (Leviticus 19.19)

There are more examples. But, this is enough to get us started. Most conservative Christians I know condemn homosexuality as an abominable practice - often while eating their sausage gravy! So, is this cherry-picking the Old Testament for verses you agree with?

These are fair questions. Leviticus speaks against tattoos (Leviticus 19.28). But, in the minds of many believers, the tattoos, shellfish, spiritism, and wearing a blended shirt are somehow non-binding but homosexuality is. How can this be? Dispensationalism has an answer for this – and I believe the only exegetically sound way of consistently providing an answer to this dilemma.

Let's compare the dispensational and the covenantal approach to understand how each seeks to interpret the text.

The Covenantal Approach

Covenant theologians answer these differences by breaking the law into three separate parts. We are told about the ceremonial, the civil, and the moral law. The ceremonial aspect was fulfilled with Jesus. The civil law was only for Israel. The moral law is for everyone. I heard this growing up – perhaps you did as well. In the words of some over-zealous Bible students, "That'll preach!" But, is it biblical?

There are problems with the idea of dividing a covenant that is described as an indivisible unit. OK, who gets to determine which part is non-moral? If all of these laws stem from the Lawgiver, does He bring forth amoral laws? At first glance, this approach, while making sense on the surface, introduces a subjectivity to the text.

101

With this method, it is now the interpreter who is deciding what is moral, what is civil, and what is ceremonial. Biblically, there is no objective way to make those distinctions.

A bigger problem is that no Israelite would understand a "three-fold" law. Neither did James in the New Testament! See James 2.10. It is always the "*law*" of Moses and not the *laws* of Moses. The Old Testament law was one single unit without ability to be arbitrarily subdivided.

How we view the law (and the believer's relationship to it) has great bearing on our view of sanctification.

This difference is not inconsequential. For how we view the law (and the believer's relationship to it) has great bearing on our view of sanctification. Taking their cue from Calvin, those within Reformed Theology hold that the law's third (and primary) use was for the sanctification of the believers.[74]

Yet, a dispensationalist is dogmatic that a believer is not under any part of the law. Consider Paul's exposition of the law and sin in Romans 7. His letter provides its own sermon illustration. To paraphrase, Paul says something like this:

> You know what it's like when two people have been married for a long time? Eventually, one of them dies and the other becomes a widow/er. No matter how long they were married or how much they loved each other, there is no obligation that the living one has toward the departed.

---

[74] John Calvin, *Institutes of the Christian Religion*, 2.7.12.

Death has concluded that relationship. In like manner, because our old man died in Christ, we have no obligation to the law. Death has freed us from it.

This is Paul's argument. The believer, as described in Romans 6, is not "under the law." But Paul provides another illustration that is damaging to the covenantal view of a three-fold law. Paul states that he would not have known coveting except the law had said, "Thou shalt not covet." At issue here is that this part of the law is part of the so-called "moral law." Paul is not under any of the law.

The Dispensational Approach

Dispensationalism takes a different approach to this. Rather than invent an artificial hermeneutical tool (a three-fold law), dispensationalists look to the Scripture. It takes an exegetical approach rather than an eisegetical one. Consider this colorful rebuttal to the concept of a three-fold division by Metcalfe:

> What! Rend asunder the one law of God into three mutilated parts, inventing the names moral, judicial, and ceremonial, just so that you can discard two and retain one? But what God has joined together, let not man put asunder. The law, one law, as such, was given by Moses. Then either we are under it, or we are not under it. It is impossible for anyone to be under only a part of it. ... God called the whole, the law. Israel calls it the law. And so did Paul, agreeing with Israel, the Jews, and the Lord Jesus, none of whom allowed of this dismemberment. It is the law, integrally, the whole of it, all that Moses commanded, and none of it can be separated from any other part of it.[75]

---

[75] John Metcalfe, *Deliverance from the Law: The Westminster Confession Exploded* (John Metcalfe Publishing Trust, 1992), 5-8.

Those who read Metcalfe need no translation! His words are clear and pointed. From a dispensational point of view, we can't read the Scripture saying, "You are not under the law" and translate that as "We are not under two-thirds of the law." Either the law has been abolished or it is in force.

As Paul described Jesus' work on Calvary and its effect on the law, his language was not vague. Writing to the Ephesians, he said that Jesus "abolished in his flesh the enmity, even the law of commandments contained in ordinances..." (Eph 2.15). Writing around the same time to the church at Colossae, he challenged them to consider how Jesus had blotted "out the handwriting or ordinances that was against us, which was contrary to us, and took it out of the way, nailing it to his cross," (Col 2.14).

Note that Paul uses descriptive terms. The law has been *abolished*, a word that implies being rendered inoperative, made powerless, invalidated. He tells us the law has been *blotted out*, a word that paints the picture of being erased, removed, wiped clean. How much clearer could Paul make it than saying "...for ye are not under the law, but under grace," in Romans 6.14-15?

These verses make it black and white, cut and dry. But, rather than answering questions, it raises some. If we are not under the law, can we live a "lawless" life under grace? Does grace empower what the Bible describes on the one hand as lasciviousness (a sexual indulgence that is unrestrained by morality) or on the other hand as Christian liberty so-called (some today use grace as their license to live less than a holy, separated life)?

Paul answers this in Romans 6.1 with a hearty, "God forbid!" Why is he so dogmatic? Because our old man died – the man who wanted to live that lifestyle. Now we have the nature of God, indwelt by the Holy Spirit, a new creation. We are "dead to sin."

Illustrations

I can see the wheels turning! "Let me get this straight: 1) I'm not under the law. 2) I'm under grace. 3) I have a new nature and my want-to's have changed. I get all of that. But even if I don't want to – it's still morally wrong to murder! Why is that so if the law has been truly done away with?"

Those are fair questions. Actually, it's at the core of this discussion of carryovers versus a clean break. Notice that murder is not wrong because the Ten Commandments say so. Murder is wrong because man is made in the image of God and to attack God's image is an attempted attack on God (Genesis 9.6).

Consider the first murder. With whom was Cain upset – Abel or God? He was upset with God and took out his anger on God's image. This was wrong even with no Mosaic Covenant. Question: Was man only in God's image under the law and today we are not? Of course not. So, the reason against murder before the law and during the law is the same after the law is fulfilled.

Let's take another example, one that is near and dear to my group of Christians – the Baptists. Let's talk about food! Where two or three are gathered together, bring a casserole! Seriously, does the Bible show any differences in what man's allowable diet was? Sure. In the Garden, there were no meat-eaters. No carne asada, no hamburgers, no rib-eyes. (Could this be a partial explanation for the Fall of Adam?!)

But as you read the Scriptures, this didn't stay the same. After the flood, God grants Noah and his family permission to eat all kinds of flesh / meat. There are NO restrictions. So, Noah was allowed to eat things that Adam could not eat before him. Yet (and this is an important observation), he was also allowed to eat non-kosher food that David would not be allowed to eat after him!

Further, those kosher laws were removed in the New Testament. What God calls clean, we can't call unclean. Paul instructed his disciples that all food was sanctified with prayer (1 Tim 4.3). Here's the principle: when one reads the Bible, it has a way of self-explaining what is followed in each dispensation. We didn't consult any commentaries to talk about murder or diet. Rather, we just read the Scriptures in its normal, historical and grammatical context.

Randy White provides some insightful questions to contemplate while studying the Scriptures in relation to this issue:

1. Is our understanding based upon anecdotal evidence of Scripture? The Philistines sent back the Ark of God on milk cows with golden mice as an offering - we shouldn't do it that way! Peter raised someone from the dead. Just because someone did it somewhere, one time, at one location doesn't make it normative Christianity. We don't get our practices and doctrines from illustrations or anecdotes.

2. Is the only teaching found in the Mosaic Law? If a principle isn't mentioned before the law or after the law - then we proceed with caution.

3. Is the teaching in the law also found before the law? For example, some believers today want a loophole for non-tithing by saying, "That was under the law." Yet, it actually predates the law, and was continued after the law as well.

4. Is this a moral demand based upon the character of God? If so, then God's character doesn't change with dispensations. This question is a companion to number 2. If something is

only mentioned in the Law, but, it is a moral demand that is rooted in the character of God – then we should take note.

5. Is it stated again in the New Testament, preferably Paul's writings? An example here is that nine of the ten commandments are repeated for New Testament believers. The one that is not repeated is "Remember the Sabbath Day." According to Exodus 32, the Sabbath was a sign for *Israel* – and the church is not Israel.[76]

Ryrie addresses the idea of carryovers as well.[77] In fact, he believes we must anticipate and expect this. In Genesis 3.15, as the dispensation of conscience begins, God promises that a Redeemer would come. This promise was not fulfilled during this dispensation, nor during the dispensations of government, patriarchs, or law.

The prophecies made under the law about the Messiah setting up a kingdom were not fulfilled in law, or grace. Those will be fulfilled during the kingdom. Those promises have carried over and were not annulled by a dispensational change.

Continuity or Discontinuity

Dispensationalism is generally listed as a system of discontinuity due to its distinction between Israel and the Church. Continuity refers to a continuation, or carryover, from an Old Testament concept into the New Testament. Discontinuity deals with a disconnect, or a change, between the testaments.

---

[76] Randy White, "The Dispensational Principle of Carryover, Part 2" https://dispensationalpublishing.com/the-dispensational-principle-of-carryover-part-2/.

[77] Ryrie, *Dispensationalism*, 56-57.

Even though dispensationalism is a discontinuity system, Michael Vlach has noted at least eight areas where there is continuity between the testaments.

1. The storyline that is prophesied in the Old Testament finds its fulfillment in Jesus Christ.
2. The coming kingdom is consistent with the kingdom promised in the Old Testament.
3. Israel, in both testaments, refer to the ethnic descendants of Abraham, Isaac, and Jacob.
4. The Day of the Lord as described in the Old Testament prophets is taught in the New Testament as well.
5. The Promised Land and Jerusalem are still significant post-Old Testament times.
6. In both testaments, salvation is extended to Gentiles.
7. Salvation is always by grace through faith.
8. The New Testament writers never give an Old Testament passage a new meaning.[78]

While we can get busy trying to dissect all the differences, let's not forget to emphasize the similarities as well. God has not scrapped the Old Testament, and called it a failure. God will continue to work His plan that was promised to Israel long ago.

As Bible readers, we take our cue from the text. What is God requiring of man during that current administration? Relationships go through stages where the administering of those relationships look differently over time. When we were first married, we ate out more than we probably should have. When children came, the managing of the house looked different. When kids started school,

---

[78] Vlach, http://mikevlach.blogspot.com/2016/12/dispensationalism-and-continuity.html.

the management changed again. When kids started driving, again, the management of the house changed again. When kids got married and started having kids - it all changed!

We never posted a sign, "The Management is Now Changing the Rules of the House." It was natural, organic and observable by any who was watching. In like manner, God doesn't post neon signs about dispensational shifts. But, as with any household, the management shift is natural, organic, and observable.

The Law of Christ

To not be "under the law" is not an invitation to lawlessness. When a Christian says he is not under the law, he means the law "of Moses." He is still under law - just not the one given by Moses. Paul tells us that when we carry one another's burdens, we fulfill the "law of Christ" (Galatians 6.2).

Christ, as a King, has an expected code to follow in His kingdom. The carryovers from each dispensation that are still applicable to believers today are collectively referred to as the law of Christ. We don't have to artificially subdivide the law of Moses into three parts; we simply let the New Testament bring clarity to the picture.

The law of Christ is only discussed in Galatians 6.2 and 1 Corinthians 9.21. What, exactly, does Paul mean by this expression? By way of *interpretation*, Paul has discussed the "law of love" in Galatians 5.13-15. This law of love aligns with what Jesus said during His earthly ministry. He gave a new commandment - that we love one another (John 13.34; 15.12). We fulfill the "law of Christ" as we love one another.

By way of *application*, the New Testament provides principles in which the New Testament believer submits to the headship (Lordship) of Christ. Why do we not kill? Well, under the law of

Christ, we "love" each other. Why we do not bear false witness? Again, under the law of Christ, this is grounded in the fact that we love each other. Why do we not steal? Because we love one another as ourselves. Paul gives a classic discourse on the power and behavior of love in 1 Corinthians 13.

In the book of Galatians, Paul is contrasting Christ's call to love and grace with the Judaizer's message of law and works. There is some irony in Paul's appeal. It is as if he is saying, "OK, I've tried to tell you that you do not need to follow the law. IF you are going to insist, then don't follow the law *of Moses*. Instead, follow the law *of Christ*."

Ryrie speaks to this thought of the law of Christ as well:

> The Mosaic law has been done away in its entirety as a code...In its place He has introduced the law of Christ. Many of the individual commands within that law are new, but some are not. Some of the ones which are old were also found in the Mosaic law and they are now incorporated completely and [are] forever done away. As part of the law of Christ they are binding on the believer today.[79]

We could say that the law of Christ "is the law of the Church Age that includes all of God's eternal law summarized as the great commandment of Matthew 22.37-40."[80]

Rather than saying the Law of Moses should be broken into moral, ceremonial, and civil – we can say that the Mosaic Law includes God's eternal moral laws built into it. These same eternal

---

[79] Charles Ryrie, "The End of the Law," *Bibliotheca Sacra* 124 (July-September, 1967): 246.

[80] Paul Schmidtbleicher, "Law in the New Testament," *Chafer Theological Journal* 09:02 (Fall 2003): 50-79.

laws are applicable to the New Testament believer and referred to as the law of Christ.

Summary

Within dispensationalism, a key component would have to include the idea of stewardship and the managing of a household. Implied within this stewardship relationship are the concepts of *time, testing*, and *truth*. While stewardship includes areas such as personal finance, we have seen that the biblical picture includes much more than just this.

While we are not under the law of Moses, this does not mean we can advocate for lawlessness. We are still under the law of Christ. Dispensationalists view the law of Moses as a single entity based upon how it was understood by the nation of Israel as well as James. On the contrary, covenantalists arbitrarily break down the law into three components.

While dispensationalism is a system of discontinuity, there are still elements of continuity within it. In areas where the New Testament introduces a clean break from a previous teaching, we are emphasizing *discontinuity*. In areas where there are carry overs from one dispensation to another, we are emphasizing *continuity*.

The Law of Christ is the rule of conduct for New Testament believers. It is built upon Christ's new commandment to love one another as well as the eternal (continuity) moral principles of God.

Chapter 5

THERE IS A DIFFERENCE

*Dispensationalism and Covenant Theology
are mutually exclusive systems*

"The great need across evangelicalism is exposition of the Scriptures...It may not be popular, it may not build mega-churches, but it will fulfill that to which they are called upon to do in ministry." J. Dwight Pentecost

Chapter Aims

1. Articulate why differences exist between Dispensationalism and Covenant Theology.
2. Explain key differences between these two systems in the areas of hermeneutics, the church, and salvation.

Introduction

I find it helpful at the beginning of each chapter to remind us where we've been. As a guide, I also want to point out where we are going. We have tried to give clear definitions to some of the more important terms. Why is this? Well, simply put, definitions are essential to having a healthy discussion. We might say that they are the only means by which we can even communicate clearly at all.

Earlier, we took a whirlwind history tour. To me, that chapter isn't simply filler-material. It adds a context of dispensationalism's place in history and its contributions to theology. Understanding the historical roots of a theological system can provide a framework for evaluating it. However, the ultimate test of any system is its fidelity to the Scriptures.

Most recently, we looked at how to identify these shifts within dispensations. What do we look for when God is administrating His house (His *oikos*) differently? Because of the principle of progressive revelation versus cumulative revelation, we observed how that affects the way we read the Bible.

Over the course of the next two chapters, it's time to make some comparisons and contrasts between two American theological giants: 1) Dispensationalism, and 2) Covenant Theology. So, let's figure out how each of these compare to each other. Specifically, in this chapter we provide an overview of each. Secondly, we need to see how each system differs in the areas of hermeneutics, the church, and salvation.

What is Covenant Theology?

Covenant Theology is a theological framework that was systematized about 100 years before Dispensationalism. As a system, both are relatively young – and adherents for both systems find warrant for their beliefs earlier in history as well.

Because Dispensationalism and Covenant Theology are often compared and contrasted, in this section it's helpful to point out what Covenant Theology teaches and how Dispensationalism is different. In the words of Renald Showers' book, we will find that "there really is a difference."

The primary differences can be found within the realm of hermeneutics and priority of the Testaments. Have you ever

114

wondered how two different people can read the exact same passage and come to two totally different conclusions on what it means? Obviously, it can't mean two contradictory truths at the same time! What's going on? When the Bible is viewed through different lens, conflicting interpretations arise.

Here's a classic example: Ask people a simple question, "Who did Jesus die for?" – and then watch people use the Bible to teach two contradictory positions. One says, "He died for the world," while another says, "He died for the church / the elect." These questions of hermeneutics make a difference.

Consider another simple question: "Can you lose your salvation?" Again, watch as different people use the same Bible to give conflicting answers. "No, salvation can never be lost - it's *eternal* life." Or, "When one reads Hebrews, it becomes evident that salvation can be lost – look at Judas." Or, "I can't lose it and no one can take it from me – but I can give it back if I change my mind." Obviously, the Bible doesn't teach *all* these positions. So again, hermeneutics is really important. The hermeneutics of covenant theology and dispensational theology are different.

Covenant theology has many tenets to its faith. Yet, at its core, it can be recognized as a system founded upon three over-arching covenants: 1) The Covenant of Redemption, 2) The Covenant of Works, and 3) The Covenant of Grace. These three covenants are not *biblical* covenants (meaning, they are nowhere explicitly stated in Scripture like the Abrahamic, Mosaic, Davidic or New Covenant). Rather, these core covenants are best described as *theological* covenants (as they form the framework for this theological system). In the minds of covenant theologians, there is implicit evidence that these covenants exist.

In simplest terms, the covenants of redemption and grace can be visualized as phase one and phase two of God's plan of salvation. The Covenant of Redemption is alleged to have been made in eternity past between the Father and the Son. The Covenant of Grace is made within "time" between God and believers. Observe that while *grace* and *redemption* are biblical words, in no place are they described in terms of a covenant.

Dispensationalists assert that covenantalism lays its entire theological foundation on implication and inference – a much shakier foundation than direct statements of Scripture.

Ernest Pickering used the colorful illustration, "It is the feeling of many that an implication is a rather shaky plank upon which to rest so large a structure."[81]

An absence of a phrase or wording in the Bible doesn't equal an absence of a teaching.

Granted, words like *rapture* and *trinity* are not found in the Bible - so an absence of a phrase or wording doesn't equal an absence of a teaching.

Paul Enns, in his book *Handbook of Theology*, provides the following chart that should prove helpful as an overview of these three covenants.

---

[81] Ernest Pickering, "The Nature of Covenant Theology," *Central Bible Quarterly* 3, No. 4 (Winter 1960): 1-8.

CONCEPTS OF COVENANT THEOLOGY[82]

Comparison	WORKS	REDEMPTION	GRACE
Persons	With Adam	With Father & Son	With Man
Promise	Physical / Eternal life	Salvation provided for man	Eternal Life
Condition	Obedience	------	Faith
Warning	Physical Death	------	Eternal Death
Time	Eden before Fall	Eternity Past	Eden after the Fall

What's at stake?

Whether one takes a covenantal or dispensational approach has bearing on theological areas. In fact, four primary areas are affected. Stated succinctly, there are four crucial areas of doctrine where people reach different conclusions based upon whether they begin with a covenantal or dispensational hermeneutic.

The four areas of concern deal with questions about the church (ecclesiology), questions about salvation (soteriology), questions about future events (eschatology), and questions about Israel (Israelology, her place in God's purposes). These are not insignificant areas of concern.

---

[82] Paul P. Enns, *The Moody Handbook of Theology* (Chicago, IL: Moody Press, 1989), 509.

These four areas are important and thus simply cannot be glossed over. Further, these areas are results, outgrowths, of the hermeneutical process that is used. Because of their importance, these four areas are separated into two chapters. So, before looking at each area of concern, let's describe the hermeneutics (at least, briefly) for each system.

The Hermeneutical Process

As a reminder, *hermeneutics* deals with the <u>science</u> and <u>art</u> of biblical interpretation. As a science, there is a process, or a set of rules to follow. As an art, there is the ability to understand nuances, to grow in one's ability, and there are areas in which there *may* be some subjectivity.

As has already been noted, the hermeneutics of dispensational theology consists of a normal, historical-grammatical, literal approach. Sometimes, this is called the plain sense or common-sense approach. This hermeneutic isn't just utilized in narratives or historical accounts. It is also used in the prophetic sections as well.

How do we know the *right* way to interpret prophecy? Do we base it on what we observe in the present or what we observe in the past? From a covenant theological perspective, the idea that the church *replaces* Israel is offensive to some. From their perspective, it isn't one of replacement, it's one of *fulfillment*.

Other theological perspectives bring in an "already, not yet" hermeneutic. This prophecy has *already* been fulfilled partially, but *not yet* completely fulfilled. It attempts to find a middle ground. Rather than giving a black and white answer – that is, the prophecy is either fulfilled or it isn't – they add an "in-between" answer. I'm not sure that this helps solve hermeneutical issues as it leads to subjective interpretation.

When Pentecost published his book *Things to Come*, he had published a massive study on eschatology from a dispensational perspective. His mammoth work is 670 pages long - not for the faint of heart! In his book, he devotes the first four chapters to the importance of hermeneutics.[83] In writing against those who use a less-than-literal hermeneutic, Pentecost exclaimed:

> Thus, the great dangers inherent in this system [he means, the allegorical approach to prophecy] are that it takes away the authority of Scripture, leaves us without any basis on which interpretations may be tested, reduces Scripture to what seems reasonable to the interpreter, and, as a result, makes true interpretation of Scripture impossible.[84]

Bernard Ramm, in his textbook on hermeneutics, gives several reasons why the literal (normal) method of understanding words is the only way to properly understand the meaning of Scripture. These reasons can be summed up by the following three:

1. This method is the usual way to interpret any literature.
2. Any secondary meaning is still dependent upon this literal, normal usage.
3. This is the only way to control any "exegetical abuse" on Scripture, which he defines as,

> We mean all interpretation in the history of the Church and in the histories of cults which forces strange and

---

[83] The book is heavily detailed. It has thirty-three chapters, all dealing with eschatological subjects rooted in a normal, historical-grammatical hermeneutic.

[84] J. Dwight Pentecost, *Things to Come: A Study in Biblical Eschatology* (Grand Rapids: Zondervan, 1958), 6.

unbiblical meanings into Scripture by some form of
allegorical interpretation (meaning by the "allegorical" any
kind of reading into Scripture secondary or tertiary or even
quaternary meanings).[85]

It is this issue of hermeneutics which brings disagreement on
what the Bible teaches about the church and salvation. In regards to
the entirety of Scripture – prophecy included – dispensationalists
default to this normal, literal, historical-grammatical approach.

By the way, this default position – even for the prophetic
portions – is not without warrant. The dispensationalist looks to the
biblical record, at the fulfilled prophecies, and uses that as a baseline
on how to interpret the remaining prophecies still unfulfilled.

When the Old Testament prophesied that the Messiah would
be born in Bethlehem (Micah 5.2), He was literally born there.
When Isaiah prophecies that the Messiah would be in a rich man's
tomb (Isaiah 53.9), He was literally placed within the tomb of
Joseph of Arimathea. In Psalm 34.20, it's prophesied that no bones
will be broken for the Messiah – this is exactly what happened.

With this precedent, when a dispensationalist reads about a
temple in Jerusalem during the Millennial Kingdom, he has no
other option than to believe that the temple will be literally rebuilt.
When a dispensationalist reads that the Son of David will establish a
kingdom with no end (Isaiah 9.6-7) and that He will sit upon the
throne of David (Psalm 132.11-12; Isaiah 9.7; Luke 1.26-33), he
cannot accept a spiritual fulfillment that Jesus has already done that.
People may disagree with the conclusion, but they can't fault us for
inconsistency here. This is where the hermeneutical process takes us.

---

[85] Bernard Ramm, *Protestant Biblical Interpretation: A Textbook of
Hermeneutics*, Third Revised Edition. (Grand Rapids: Baker, 1970), 124.

In contrast, the covenant theological approach is *mostly* normal, literal-historical-grammatical as well. I have been greatly edified by non-dispensational preachers expounding the text. We may disagree, but we're not enemies. When it comes to unfulfilled prophecies, we part ways. All of a sudden, prophecies *made to Israel* are being fulfilled *by the church*. Based upon God's method of fulfilling prophecies previously, dispensationalists simply cannot accept these conclusions.

So, with a brief explanation about hermeneutics, let's see how this works out with each respective system in relation to key doctrines. In this chapter, we specifically focus on the biblical understanding of the church and of salvation.

Questions about the Church

When it comes to the doctrine of the church, competing views exist between that of the dispensationalist and that of the covenantalist. Both read the same Bible. Yet, they read it differently. As a result, they will always come to conflicting positions. Both views cannot be correct.

In studying the differences between the two, McCune observed that "Covenant Theology places the church's beginning usually with Adam or Abraham, and it places the church's final composition or end with the second coming of Christ..."[86] To be fair, McCune is not a Covenant Theologian. Perhaps his perspective may be skewed or biased because of his dispensational theology. So, what have those who embrace covenant theology said about the church's origin?

---

[86] Rolland McCune, *A Systematic Theology of Biblical Christianity*, Vol. 3 (Detroit: Detroit Baptist Theological Seminary, 2010), 213.

Wayne Grudem makes the following statement in his definition of church:

> *The church is the community of all true believers for all time.*
> This definition understands the church to be made of all
> those who are truly saved. Paul says, "Christ loved *the church*
> and gave himself up for her" (Eph. 5:25). Here the term
> "the church" is used to apply to all those whom Christ died
> to redeem, all those who are saved by the death of Christ.
> But that must include all true believers for all time, both
> believers in the New Testament age and believers in the
> Old Testament age as well.[87]

In case Grudem is in danger of being misunderstood, he clarifies in an explanatory footnote from the quotation: "In this book I have taken a **non-dispensational** position on this question..." In context, the question is, "What constitutes a church?" From Grudem's perspective, the church includes all saints from all time. Why? The reason he gives in this text is because "Christ died for the church." It is as if Grudem's theological spectacles sees the word *only* in Ephesians 5.25.

However, if we were to take this logic to its extreme, the results become ridiculous. Paul (yes, the same Paul who wrote Ephesians 5) wrote in Galatians 2 that Jesus loved him and "gave himself for me." Surely no one would say that Jesus *only* died for Paul! How does a dispensationalist handle the question raised by Ephesians 5?

1. Jesus died for all, the world (1 John 2.1-2; John 3:16, 1 Timothy 2.5, 4.10, etc)

---

[87] Wayne Grudem, *Systematic Theology: An Introduction to Biblical Doctrine* (Grand Rapids: Zondervan Pub. House, 2004), 853.

2. Jesus died for the church, which is a part of the world
   (Ephesians 5; John 10)
3. Jesus died for Paul, who is part of the church and also part of
   the world (Galatians 2).

There is no contradiction here. The New Testament writers do not use the terms "world" and "church" interchangeably any more than they use the words "Israel" and "church" interchangeably. The context of what was written determines the scope of Christ's death that was discussed. It is valid to say Jesus died for the world, for the church, and for Paul without ever having to resort to saying the church (which Paul describes was a mystery in Ephesians 3) existed in the Old Testament.

Consider the implications of these differences concerning whether the church begins with Adam (or Abraham) or at Pentecost.

If the church began with Adam, then from Adam until now, there has only been one people of God. If there is only one people of God, then there is more continuity between the testaments than discontinuity. If today's believers are part of the same body as Abraham, then the covenants made to Abraham apply to them. Hence, there is no real distinction between the Church and the nation of Israel.

When I first started serving in ministry (as a volunteer on a Sunday school bus route), I taught the children a song that I had learned. Obviously, all children's songs and choruses have been scripturally tested, right? Here were the words:

Every promise in the book is mine. Every chapter, every verse, every line. All these blessings of His love divine. Every promise in the book is mine.

One promise says that descendants will be like the stars of the sea and sands of the shore. Is that for me? I read someone is made into a great nation. Is that me? I read where the holy land has been promised to someone – is that for me? I'm being facetious here! Not *every* promise is to me. Some promises are *specifically* Jewish and to interpret them any other way is to do a disservice to the text.

What has been described as the covenant understanding of the origin of the church is in opposition to the way dispensationalism understands its origin. For a dispensationalist, the concept of the church involves a called-out (the word *ecclesia* is a compound word that can mean "called-out") assembly of believers that are the body of Christ. This was not revealed in the Old Testament, but was a mystery. If it was a mystery, how did it exist during that time?

What does Dispensationalism teach about the Church?

Dispensationalism approaches the entire Bible through the lens of progressive revelation. God did not reveal His truth *en toto*. Mark how the law would have been a mystery to Noah. It wasn't that the law wasn't <u>understood</u> by Noah - it was <u>unknown</u>. Why was it unknown? It had not been revealed yet.

Progressive revelation is linked to the hermeneutical approach utilized by Dispensationalists. The approach is to study Scripture through the paradigm of normal, literal, historical and grammatical means. Due to a consistent use of this approach, dispensationalism finds no mention of the church in the Old Testament – not one. Why is traditional dispensationalism dogmatic on this issue?

Reardon notes the following in one of his articles:

> Mystery is the central theological concept to grasp in Paul's presentation of the stewardship that had been entrusted to him. He was commissioned by God to reveal the sacred secret that had been maintained throughout the whole OT but had now been revealed

in Christ through Paul (Eph. 3:1-13). The term occurs three times in this crucial passage (vv. 3, 4, 9).[88]

How we define the word *mystery* is crucial. Is the word to imply something *unknown* or something *not understood*. For Covenant Theologians, the church existed in the Old Testament, it was just not as fully understood as it is today. Dispensationalists maintain that the concept of a church was unknown in the Old Testament, and cite as proof the words of Paul:

> For this cause I Paul, the prisoner of Jesus Christ for you Gentiles, If ye have heard of the dispensation of the grace of God which is given me to you-ward: How that by revelation he made known unto me the mystery; (as I wrote afore in few words, Whereby, when ye read, ye may understand my knowledge in the mystery of Christ), Which in other ages was not made known unto the sons of men, as it is now revealed unto his holy apostles and prophets by the Spirit; That the Gentiles should be fellowheirs, and of the same body, and partakers of his promise in Christ by the gospel; Whereof I was made a minister, according to the gift of the grace of God given unto me by the effectual working of his power. (Ephesians 3.1-7)

Notice Paul received this mystery by *revelation* - a truth that was previously unknown and otherwise unknowable. He specifically states that in previous ages this truth was not made known unto the

---

[88] Parker Reardon, "Dispensationalism 101 - Part 3," http://dispensationalpublishing.com/issues-of-contention-part-1-ecclesiology-and-eschatology/.

125

son of men. It has now been revealed to the apostles and prophets through communication from the Spirit.

What is the new truth that Paul received (of which, he was a steward)? Was it that Gentiles should be included into the plan of redemption? No. For we already see this in the Old Testament time and again. This new truth was that Gentiles would be brought into the same body by the Gospel. What body are believers made part of at salvation? We are placed "in Christ" (again, a position that was unknown before the apostles received that mystery.

Definition of church

We should stop for a moment and define *church*. The simple definition of "called-out assembly" isn't specific enough. That would describe a sporting event or three people in the International Space Station! Here's why getting the definition is so important – as long as a "church" is *only* a called-out assembly, then obviously Israel becomes a "church" in the Old Testament. She becomes as much of a church as the 90,000 people being called out of Knoxville and its surrounding areas to watch a University of Tennessee football game!

Etymologically, we receive our English word *church* from the Scottish word *kirk* (and the German *kirche*).

> "Aye, lassie, 'twas pure barry, it 'twas. I dinnae ken
> that I ever heard a better sermon at kirk!"

That sentence above may be fun to say, but it doesn't really *define* the concept yet. To take it back a bit, both the Scots and the Germans have derived their words from the Greek *kuriakon*, the neuter adjective of *kurios* ("Lord"), meaning "belonging to the Lord."[89] Think about it – every time we say we are going to church,

---

[89] Paul Enns, *Handbook of Theology* (Chicago: Moody, 1989), 346–347.

126

we are subconsciously reminding ourselves that we are going to a place that belongs to the Lord.

Of course, this understanding of a word's history hasn't really helped us much! If the "earth is the Lord's" according to the Psalmist, we just made the whole world a church! We need a working definition that helps us identify what a biblical church is. There are variations offered by theologians. Here is a simple definition we can get our minds wrapped around:

> The church is a gathering of those who believe in Jesus Christ as Savior and Lord, who are committed to meet [assemble] regularly for worship, teaching, fellowship, and prayer and are committed to making disciples of all people (or, who follow the Great Commission).

We can expand this definition by including that they observe the two ordinances of baptism and the Lord's Supper (Communion). Some may include that they are led by a pastor. James Boice recognizes that this group thus described is different from the nation of Israel in the Old Testament:

> The church has characteristics that cannot rightly be applied to the Old Testament assembly and which therefore set it off as something new. The church is (1) founded on the Lord Jesus Christ, (2) is called into being by the Holy Spirit, and (3) is to contain people of all races who thereby become one new people in the sight of God.[90]

Using the New Testament as a guide, Jesus said that He would build *His* church (Matthew 16.18). He is the *Head* and the church is *His Body*. This church was a mystery in the Old Testament (Eph 3;

---

[90] James Boice, *Foundations of the Christian Faith: A Comprehensive and Readable Theology* (Downers Grove: InterVarsity, 2019), 584.

Col 1). Since it was both unknown and unrevealed to the nation of Israel, then, even with superficial similarities, it must still be something different.

When did it begin?

Concerning the origin of the church, a dispensationalist and covenantalist come to different positions as well. They both teach different things. From a covenant perspective, with only one people of God with one plan - the church existed as far back as Adam. This position requires a different *definition* and *understanding* of what constitutes a church.

A dispensationalist studies the New Testament and he can't help but notice that something big happened at Jerusalem during the Feast of Pentecost. Here's Ryrie's take on this:

> Pentecost marks the beginning of the church as a functioning body by the outpouring of the Spirit...[91]

Millard Erickson agrees with this notion as well. Clearly, he states, "We conclude the church originated in Pentecost."[92] Stanley Toussaint uses Peter's use of *beginning* in Acts 11:15 (which cross-

---

[91] Charles Ryrie, *Basic Theology: A Popular Systematic Guide to Understanding Biblical Truth* (Chicago: Moody, 1986), 466. For those who pinpoint the origin of the church within Christ's ministry, I like Ryrie's emphasis on a "functioning" body...It may have existed prior (Ryrie doesn't say), but it functioned differently after Pentecost.

[92] Millard Erickson, *Christian Theology* (Grand Rapids: Baker, 1998), 1058. Note that Erickson is not a dispensationalist, and though he states a dispensational truth, he is not consistent as he believes the OT saints were incorporated into this church at Pentecost.

references back to Acts 1:5) in reference to the baptizing work of the Spirit as the beginning of the church age.[93]

In recounting what happened next, Peter made an important identification of the day of Pentecost with the Lord's prediction of Spirit baptism (1:4–5). Luke did not state specifically in chapter 2 that Pentecost was that fulfillment, but Peter here pointedly said so by the phrase at the beginning (cf. 10:47, "just as we have," and 11:17, "the same gift as He gave us"). The Church Age, then, began on the day of Pentecost.[94]

This difference of whether the church was in the Old Testament or after Pentecost has some theological implications. One's understanding of the commencement of the church will bring about a different view of how a person becomes a member of the church as well. Because covenantal understanding sees the church and Israel through the lens of continuity, Reformed (Covenant) churches generally practice infant baptism.

The subject of infant baptism (pedo-baptism) brings together good people who both affirm and deny its validity. From a Covenant perspective, an infant, as a child, was circumcised and thus made part of the covenant community. From a Dispensational perspective, adults (not infants) were baptized. The concerns for baptism included the authority of the one baptizing, the profession of the one being baptized, and the mode in which it was conducted.

Concerning authority, dispensationalists believe that the authority to baptize is an ordinance given by the Head to His churches. Baptism is reserved only for believers, those old enough to

---

[93] Acts 1.5 prophesies about Pentecost coming in the near future. Acts 11:15 points back to this event as "the beginning." Toussaint and others say that this "beginning" was the beginning of the church.

[94] Stanley Toussaint, *Acts* in The Bible Knowledge Commentary (Wheaton, IL: Victor, 1983), 2: 349-432.

give a personal profession of salvation. The mode, biblically, was always by immersion (as opposed to sprinkling or pouring). Covenant theology attaches a different significance to baptism.

Note that in a non-covenantal church, believers are added based upon their personal testimony, agreement with the church's doctrine, and a willingness to have followed in believer's baptism. However, in a covenantal church, no personal testimony is required. An infant, through no decision of its own, is joined to the church. This issue was a major disagreement that the Reformers had with the Anabaptists:

> To the Reformers the denial of baptism to infants literally damned them—even the Zwinglians and Calvinists who denied the sacramental power of baptism believed that the rejection of infant baptism excluded the child from the nurture and fellowship of God' s people. To Luther that denial was blasphemy— a rejection of a power of God to act redemptively in a manner of His own choosing, through the Word and water of baptism. This issue separated the Anabaptists from Christian fellowship and community in the eyes of all of the Reformers.[95]

Granted, both a non-covenantalist and a covenantalist appreciate the importance of the church. Both would admonish their followers to not forsake that assembling. Both would give themselves to reading the Word and observing the Lord's table.

Yet, in fairness, we have to at least notice that the church is understood differently by both as well. A few of these differences

---

[95] John Oyer, "Sticks and Stones Broke Their Bones, and Vicious Names Did Hurt Them!," *Christian History Magazine-Issue 5: Radical Reformation: The Anabaptists* (Worcester, PA: Christian History Institute, 1985).

have been discussed here simply to show that people reading the same text come to different conclusions based upon their hermeneutical starting points.

Allow this reference chart to highlight the differences in ecclesiology between Dispensationalism and Covenant Theology.

Differing Views on the Church

	Dispensationalism	Covenant Theology
Definition	*Called-out assembly who follow Jesus, meet for worship and fellowship, and depart to obey Great Commission*	*Called-out assembly*
Beginning of Church	*At Pentecost*	*In the OT*
Definition of *Mystery*	*Concept not revealed; unknown*	*Concept not fully understood*
Church's relation to Israel	*Distinct*	*Church is an outgrowth of Israel*
View on Baptism	*For believers only*	*Infants are baptized to identify with the Covenant*

Questions about Salvation

Covenant theology approaches all of Scripture through the paradigm of a theological covenant. Remember, previously we discussed *theological* covenants versus *biblical* covenants. A biblical covenant is one explicitly stated in Scripture.

131

The Bible mentions the Mosaic Covenant (Law, Law of Moses, etc), the Abrahamic Covenant, Land Covenant, Davidic Covenant and the New Covenant. Neither the Covenant Theologian nor the Dispensationalist would deny that these covenants exist. These are clearly provided throughout the Old Testament in multiple places.

The Covenant theologian builds a theological covenant framework that he feels is implied in Scripture. These covenants are constructed logically and then contribute to his understanding of Scripture. The Covenant of Works, which would have been God's way for Adam to be saved / enjoy God's fellowship before the Fall, was short-lived. Yet, there was another covenant, a hidden and mysterious one, in which God covenanted within the Godhead to bring His chosen to enjoy fellowship with Him forever.

This covenant, sometimes referred to as the Covenant of Grace or Redemption, was made in eternity past. God the Father would elect (choose) a finite number of Adam's descendants for salvation. God the Son agreed to pay for the sins of these elect (and their sins alone). God the Spirit's role was to apply the atoning work of the cross to these elect people.

This understanding has practical applications. For example, Jay Adams, sometimes called the Father of Nouthetic Counseling, admits his theology affects his counseling. Notice what he states in *Competent to Counsel*:

> As a reformed Christian, the writer believes that counselors must not tell any unsaved counselee that Christ died for him, for they cannot say that. No man knows except Christ himself who are his elect for whom he died.[96]

---

[96] Jay Adams, *Competent to Counsel: Introduction to Nouthetic Counseling* (Grand Rapids: Ministry Resources Library, 1986), 70.

Adams is being consistent with his theology. The teaching of the Covenant of Grace is fleshed out more in a Calvinistic soteriology. Calvinism teaches its view of salvation through the acrostic TULIP:

1. T - Total Depravity
2. U - Unconditional Election
3. L - Limited Atonement
4. I - Irresistible Grace
5. P - Perseverance of the Saints[97]

This is not the context to discuss the merits / demerits of each of these thoughts, but a familiarity with the acrostic at least provides understanding. A covenantalist will *always* have a Calvinistic soteriology because of his belief in the theological covenants of grace and redemption.

This understanding of a limited atonement and a specifically elected people who can be saved is inherent in the covenant view - it is not mandated by a dispensational view.

From a covenant view, God has one plan of salvation for all of His covenant (elected) people since Adam. This demonstration of saving grace is just the outworking of the one eternal covenant of grace. Further, all believers from the Old Testament would have placed their faith in Christ. Charles Hodge describes this position as a covenant theologian:

> ...It was not the mere trust of faith in God, or simple piety, which was required [for salvation] but faith in

---

[97] In full disclosure, I reject Calvinism in its entirety. I affirm total depravity, but do not define it as total inability. I believe the Bible teaches election; but I view this as pointing toward glorification rather than justification. Much more could be said but this is not the place.

the promised redeemer, or faith in the promised
redemption through the Messiah.[98]

Yet, even covenant theologians understand the limitations the
Old Testament brings to this issue. Observe how Hodge had
appealed to "supplementary instruction" and "divine illumination"
just a few pages earlier.[99] Both of these sources are outside the
Scriptural domain (which is our final source of authority in matters
of faith and practice). Notice the recognition admitted by covenant
theologian, J. Barton Payne:

> That, to satisfy God, God must die, that men might
> inherit God, to be with God was incomprehensible
> under the Old Testament seminal knowledge of the
> Trinity, the incarnation, and the crucifixion followed
> by the resurrection.[100]

For a dispensationalist, God has only one plan of salvation as
well. However, this belief has at times been misunderstood. Perhaps
due to an inability for some to articulate this position clearly or
because of some inexact statements made in some dispensational
books, some have accused dispensationalism of teaching multiple
ways of salvation.

> Even before the Scofield Reference Bible became so
> popular, the notion that God chose different ways of saving
> sinners at different times in man's history was rife. Under

---

[98] Charles Hodge, *Systematic Theology* (Grand Rapids: Eerdmans,
1981), 2:372.

[99] Hodge, 2:367.

[100] J. Barton Payne, *An Outline of Hebrew History* (Grand Rapids:
Baker, 1954), 222.

this notion – known as Dispensationalism – the world is seen as a household administered by God at several stages of revelation, each stage placing on man the obligation to respond to his plan as revealed at any given particular period. Some distinguish his plan for Israel from his plan for the Church. More commonly, others claim to see seven or more ways of saving sinners, each differing from its predecessor![101]

These words are not an isolated incident. Clarence Bass makes the same assertion by claiming that the logical conclusion of dispensational soteriology would "inevitably result in multiple forms of salvation – that men are not saved the same way in all ages."[102]

Despite some claims to the contrary, dispensationalism doesn't teach that Old Testament saints were saved through the sacrifices, through the law, or through other meritorious works. Many covenant theologians acknowledge that this has been a strawman accusation with no basis in actual dispensational teaching. In fact, Vern Poythress, a vocal critic of dispensationalism, never levels this accusation in his book.[103]

By the way, the dispensationalist could turn the tables here and say, "Actually, it's the covenantal understanding that teaches two ways of salvation." What? Sure, listen to R.C. Sproul discuss the relationship God had with Adam:

_____

[101] John M. Brentnall, "Two Dispensations: One Salvation," Banner of Truth. https://banneroftruth.org/us/resources/articles/2012/two-dispensations-one-salvation/

[102] Clarence Bass, *Backgrounds to Dispensationalism* (Grand Rapids: Eerdmans, 1960), 34.

[103] Vern Poythress, *Understanding Dispensationalists* (Grand Rapids: Zondervan, 1987).

The original covenant between God and humankind was a covenant of works. In this covenant, God required perfect and total obedience to His rule. He promised eternal life as the blessing of obedience, but threatened mankind with death for disobeying God's law.[104]

Does Adam want *eternal life?* Then, he must be obedient to the law under the covenant of works. Does this not sound like salvation, in the beginning, was by works and after the Fall it was by grace? That's two ways of salvation. I'm playing devil's advocate here. I know of *no* covenant theologian who would agree with what I said! But by the same notion, I know of *no* dispensational theologian who says salvation was by more than one way either.

For the dispensationalist, salvation has always been by grace through faith. However, the object of faith has varied for different dispensations. Abraham had righteousness imputed to him because he believed the promise of God about his descendants. The Bible doesn't say that Abraham placed his faith in the finished work of Calvary. Nor did he "ask Jesus to be his Savior." Rather, God's grace was evident and Abraham's faith was just as evident. In Genesis 15, Abraham believed God and it was counted to him for righteousness.

The covenant theologian may claim that Abraham was saved by trusting in a coming Messiah based on the supplementary instruction or illumination argument. **But a dispensationalist cannot go beyond the Scriptures.**

The biblical record in Genesis 15.6 teaches that God imputed righteousness to Abraham (He justified him) when he believed the promises about his descendants. God's grace made the promise available. Abraham received it by faith. It has always been a salvation predicated upon grace and faith (Ephesians 2.8-9). Always.

---

[104]https://www.monergism.com/thethreshold/articles/onsite/covenantworks.html. R.C. Sproul, "The Covenant of Works."

Whether it be C.I. Scofield, Charles Ryrie, John Darby, or John Walvoord – **no** leader in dispensationalism has taught multiple ways of salvation. Lewis Sperry Chafer had this to say:

> Are there two ways by which one may be saved? In reply to this question it may be stated that salvation of whatever specific character is always the work of God in behalf of man and never a work of man in behalf of God. This is to assert that God never saved any one person or group of persons on any other ground than that righteous freedom to do so which the Cross of Christ secured. There is, therefore, but one way to be saved and that is by the power of God made possible through the sacrifice of Christ.[105]

While dispensationalists have taught that the content of faith has changed, the method of salvation has always been by grace through faith. It's time to burn that strawman once and for all. Let's agree that neither the dispensationalist nor the covenantalist teach multiple ways of salvation.

We may disagree on who salvation is for - but we can't disagree on how it's accomplished. It's by grace, through faith - always. Personally, as a literalist, I am able to affirm the following statements from Scripture:

God loves the world	John 3.16
Jesus is the propitiation for the world's sin	1 John 2.1-2
God will have all men to be saved	1 Timothy 4.2-6
Jesus is the Savior of all men	1 Timothy 4.10
God is not willing that any perish	2 Peter 3.9

---

[105] L.S. Chafer, "Inventing Heretics Through Misunderstanding," *Bibliotheca Sacra* 102 (Jan 1945): 1.

Summary

This chapter is not one to be read as entertainment. It requires some mental focus to be able to track the arguments. While what has been covered may not be "elemental theology" for some, I have done my best to take these major concepts and place them on the proverbial bottom shelf for all to see.

In this chapter, we've covered three "big rocks." We have observed the importance of hermeneutics and specifically, how covenantal and dispensational hermeneutics differ. We have noticed how different hermeneutical approaches affects one's view of the church, as well as one's view of salvation.

In the next chapter, we see how these differences affect one's view of Israel and end times. For now, this chart can provide a few takeaways by means of contrast:

Dispensationalism	Covenantalism
Begins with progressive revelation and the Old Testament	Begins with cumulative revelation and the New Testament
Consistently applies the normal, historical, grammatical approach to all Scripture	Applies the normal, historical, grammatical approach to most of Scripture (prophecy excluded)
The Church was a mystery that began at Pentecost	The Church existed in the Old Testament, though not fully understood
May or may not have a Calvinistic soteriology	Will always have a Calvinistic soteriology
God has a future plan for national Israel	The Church (spiritual Israel) has inherited the promises originally given to national Israel.

Chapter 6

END TIMES AND ISRAEL

Where one starts determines where one ends

"The second coming of Christ will be so revolutionary that it will change every aspect of life on this planet." Billy Graham

Chapter Aims

1. Articulate differences between Dispensationalism and Covenant Theology with respect to the areas of eschatology and Israelology.
2. Explain God's future plan for the literal nation of Israel in the near future.

Introduction

The last chapter was a bit heavy! When it comes to doctrinal areas of disagreement, it sometimes takes more than a shallow catch phrase and a great illustration to understand the issues completely. You may feel like you haven't fully grasped it all. However, at a minimum I believe you can understand that the hermeneutics that we follow makes all the difference in these discussions. As an example, we noted that a covenantalist and a dispensationalist have different views concerning the church and salvation.

I'll give you a brief warning: This chapter will have some of those same heavy elements in it as well. Why? Well, in this chapter, we observe two more doctrines where these two systems have distinctions that are important to note.

Specifically, I want to show you that dispensationalism and covenantalism have a different view concerning the end times and the future of Israel. These differences affect us as believers. To give advanced notice, if the dispensationalist hermeneutic is correct, we are raptured *before* the Tribulation. If the covenantal hermeneutic is correct, we will go *through* the Tribulation.

Putting the two systems side-by-side, let's see the differences.

Questions about End Times

Covenant theology and dispensationalism approach the subject of the prophetic portions of Scripture from different paradigms as well. Whatever these differences are, it is fair to state that each difference can be traced back to one's hermeneutics. Our eschatology is not developed in isolation from other theological disciplines.

Often, in conversations about end times, the subject of the rapture comes up. The word *rapture* is not found in the Bible (much like the word *Trinity*). Yet, as stated previously, absence of a word does not equal an absence of teaching. The word itself comes to us from the Medieval Latin *raptura*, which literally meant a seizure, a rape, or a kidnapping!

In Paul's letter to the Thessalonian church, he says that believers will be "caught up." The Latin Vulgate translates this phrase with *rapiemur*, from which our English word rapture is derived. However, the question about the rapture isn't about its etymology! Rather, the question is about its timing. Specifically, two questions need to be answered. First, for whom is the rapture? Secondly, when will this rapture take place?

For whom is the Rapture?

Concerning the *participants* in this catching away, a few minor points of contention exist within dispensationalism - and usually it is over terminology too loosely defined. First, is this the rapture of the church, as in all baptized believers who are members of local New Testament churches? Or, is it more accurate to say that this is the rapture of all believers - those who are "in Christ." In Ryrie's book on theology, he discusses the "teaching concerning the Rapture of the church."[106]

Perhaps another way to parse this difference would be to imagine a tale of two brothers. These fictional brothers illustrate a nuanced difference that some try to make in this discussion. John, the older brother, was saved at the age of nine, quickly baptized, and has been a faithful member of his church his entire life.

The younger brother, Tom, went through the school of hard knocks and wound up in prison. While in the state penitentiary, a chaplain led him to Christ. Thankfully, both brothers are now believers - but only John is involved in a church. The Rapture happens while Tom is still imprisoned. Is he left behind while his brother is caught up? Or, do both (as believers) get raptured simultaneously? Is this needless theological bantering or does the Bible answer this question clearly?

According to Hixson, "The Rapture refers to the sudden catching up of Church Age believers to meet the Lord in the air when He returns at the close of the present age."[107] Notice his

---

[106] Charles Ryrie, *Basic Theology: A Popular Systematic Guide to Understanding Biblical Truth* (Chicago, IL: Moody Press, 1999), 557.

[107] J. B. Hixson and Mark Fontecchio, *What Lies Ahead: A Biblical Overview of the End Times* (Brenham, TX: Lucid Books, 2013), 178.

defining of the term focuses on believers who are connected to the "church age" as opposed to a specific local church.

The partial rapture view teaches that only those believers who are "watching" and "waiting" for the Lord's return will be found worthy to escape the terrors of the Tribulation by being taken in the Rapture.[108] Those with this view teach that the rapture is only for the spiritual believers (and not the entirety of saved people).

The church is the *body* and the *bride* of Christ. These metaphors are theologically rich and tremendously encouraging. When a person accepts Christ today, the Holy Spirit places him "in Christ." That saved believer, before he is ever baptized or becomes a member of a local church, is in Christ. When Jesus calls us out of this world, He will not leave parts of His body behind who weren't baptized or faithfully serving in a church. The participants in the rapture are all the believers on earth when the trumpet sounds.

When should the Rapture be expected?

Concerning the *timing* of this event, the debate intensifies. The issue of timing is generally viewed through its relationship to the tribulation and the Second Coming. The rapture *is not* the Second Coming. At the Rapture, believers meet Christ *in the air*. At the Second Coming, believers come with Christ *to the earth* to set up His promised kingdom.

Typically, dispensationalists have held that the rapture would be pre-tribulational. Dispensationalists believe that there will be a seven-year period on earth known as the tribulation. This seven-year period is interchangeably known as the "time of Jacob's trouble" (Jer 30.7) and "Daniel's Seventieth Week" (Dan 9.24-27). If the dispensational understanding of the Rapture is correct, then there is

---

[108] Charles Ryrie, *Basic Theology: A Popular Systematic Guide to Understanding Biblical Truth* (Chicago, IL: Moody Press, 1999), 558.

a sense of expectancy for His soon return. Again, as Hixson states, "…imminency does not prove pretribulationism; pretribulationism demands imminency."[109]

A few caveats are in order first to provide a historical and grammatical context of this concept. What background would New Testament (Jewish) writers have had in mind as they wrote about end times? Granted, this is a brief overview, but is needed to provide the right perspective.

The Time of Jacob's Trouble: Jeremiah 30.7

In the Weeping Prophet's words, we read, "Alas! for that day *is* great, so that none *is* like it: it *is* even the time of Jacob' trouble; but he shall be saved out of it." The eschatological "day of the LORD" (that day) is referenced in this passage - which is worthy of a book-length discussion itself!

Sometimes, this "trouble" in Jeremiah 30.7 is referred to as the "birth pains" Israel will go through as she is birthed into the kingdom. This is not a novel concept with Jeremiah. Earlier, the prophet Isaiah predicted this event as well. In Isaiah 66.5-9, he discusses a *travailing*. A careful reading indicates a "birth" *before* the travailing (v.7) and a birth *after* the travailing (v9).

In fact, Matthew 24 may allude to this Jewish understanding when he discusses the "beginning of *sorrows*" in verse 8. The word *sorrow* (odin; ωδιν) is a word that distinctly describes the intense labor pains and discomfort associated with contractions.

Jeremiah says this day of Jacob's trouble is a day like no other. Daniel 12 refers to this time using similar language.

---

[109] Hixson and Fontecchio, *What Lies Ahead*, 180.

> At that time shall Michael stand up, the great prince
> which standeth for the children of thy people: **and there**
> **shall be a time of trouble, such as never was since there was a**
> **nation even to that same time:** and at that time, thy people
> shall be delivered, every one that shall be found written in
> the book. (Daniel 12.1)

Both prophets refer to a future time of trouble. Both also point out that during this time will come a great deliverance from the Lord. In the Olivet Discourse that Jesus gives just prior to His crucifixion, the same description is painted yet again.

> For then shall be great tribulation, **such as was not since**
> **the beginning of the world to this time, no, nor ever shall be.**
> And except those days should be shortened, there should no
> flesh be saved: but for the elect's sake those days shall be
> shortened. (Mt 24:21-2)

This topic, while fascinating, is tangential to the discussion of dispensationalism. Much more has been written on this subject. However, for this context, we simply note that this is the time of *Jacob's* trouble – not the time of the *church's* trouble. This end-time event that prepares Israel to receive her king is rooted in God's plan for Israel.

Daniel's Seventieth Week

In Daniel 9, the prophet lays out a prophetic calendar that covers seventy "sevens" (translated *weeks*). In our paradigm, a "week" is seven days. However, in this biblical narrative, the word is more generic, meaning simply "seven" - with context deciding whether it's seven days, seven weeks, seven men, seven years, etc.

Consider the word "dozen." Say that to some people, and immediately it is associated with Krispy Kreme donuts. For others, it's a dozen eggs. The word *dozen* simply means "twelve" and context tells the reader / the listener what twelve items are being discussed.

According to what Daniel describes, sixty-nine of the seventy weeks have already been fulfilled. Most Bible commentators view this prophecy as concerning 490 years (70 x 7). Pentecost explains the significance of this prophetic program that Daniel foresaw:

> This span of time was decreed for Daniel's people (cf. "your people" in Dan. 10:14; 11:14) and the Holy City (cf. 9:16, 24). This prophecy, then, is concerned not with world history or church history, but with the history of Israel and the city of Jerusalem. By the time these 490 years run their course, God will have completed six things for Israel. The first three have to do with sin, and the second three with the kingdom. The basis for the first three was provided in the work of Christ on the cross, but all six will be realized by Israel at the Second Advent of Christ.[110]

Thus, one week is left to fulfill (a seven-year period). Dispensationalists believe this as yet unfulfilled seven-week period is what New Testament describes as the tribulation period.

Again – a fascinating topic! And, yet again – discussing prophecy is not the goal of the book. So, in this context of dispensational eschatology, the text specifically states that "Seventy weeks are determined upon *thy* people and upon *thy* holy city." Who would be the people of Daniel? The physical descendants of Abraham, Isaac, and Jacob - it's Israel. What is the holy city for Daniel and his people? It's Jerusalem.

From Jeremiah's and Daniel's perspective, the tribulation (time of Jacob's trouble; the final seventieth week) is about *Israel / Jacob*

---

[110] J. Dwight Pentecost, "Daniel," in *The Bible Knowledge Commentary: An Exposition of the Scriptures*, ed. J. Walvoord and R. Zuck, vol. 1 (Wheaton, IL: Victor, 1985), 1361.

(the Jews) and not about the church. Thus, because of a belief in a distinction between Israel and the church (and other exegetical proofs from the Scriptures), this causes dispensationalists to be mostly (if not entirely) pre-tribulational in their view of the timing of the rapture.

If you are still tracking with this information overload, then, this means that dispensationalists believe the rapture for believers takes place *before* the tribulation begins, thus restarting God's program with Israel (which has been on hold since they rejected its king at His first coming).

What does Covenant Theology teach about the Rapture?

Starting with the priority of the Old Testament, reading the prophecies normally and literally, the hermeneutic of the dispensationalist causes him to place the rapture before the Tribulation. What do covenantalists, who are mostly normal, historical-grammatical in their approach, teach about the timing of the rapture?

The covenantal approach to end-times does not reach the same conclusion as their theological counterparts. Hear amillennial Covenant Theologian, Louis Berkhof, describe his objections to premillennialism (his objections to a premillennial view of the kingdom would also apply to a pre-tribulational rapture):

> The theory is based on a literal interpretation of the prophetic delineations of the future of Israel and of the Kingdom of God, which is entirely untenable.[111]

---

[111] Berkhof, *Systematic Theology* (Grand Rapids: Eerdmans, 1938), 712.

Notice his statement - a theory based on a literal interpretation is untenable! Berkhof continues with his hermeneutical justification for the kingdom to be spiritual, and not physical. And, his belief that we are living currently in the kingdom of God with the eternal kingdom to come precludes any need for a rapture:

> The contention that the names "Zion" and "Jerusalem" are never used by the prophets in any other than a literal sense, that the former always denotes a mountain, and the latter, a city, is clearly contrary to fact. There are passages in which both names are employed to designate Israel, the Old Testament Church of God, Isa. 49:14; 51:3; 52:1, 2. And this use of the terms passes right over into the New Testament, Gal. 4:26; Heb. 12:22; Rev. 3:12; 21:9. It is remarkable that the New Testament, which is the fulfilment of the Old, contains no indication whatsoever of the re-establishment of the Old Testament theocracy by Jesus, nor a single undisputed positive prediction of its restoration, while it does contain abundant indications of the spiritual fulfilment of the promises given to Israel, Matt. 21:43; Acts 2:29–36, 15:14–18; Rom. 9:25, 26; Heb. 8:8–13; 1 Pet. 2:9; Rev. 1:6; 5:10.[112]

Regardless on your personal view on this issue, what is undeniable is the fact that the covenant theologian and the dispensational theologian come to the text with a different hermeneutic. The dispensationalist comes wielding his normal, literal, historical-grammatical hermeneutic. The covenant theologian will accept that hermeneutic until coming to the prophetic portions of Scripture.

However, Berkhof doesn't speak for all covenant theologians. For example, R.C. Sproul, a noted covenant theologian, believes in

---

[112] Berkhof, *Systematic Theology*, 713.

the rapture. In describing his understanding of 1 Thessalonians 4, Sproul teaches that,

> Here we see that the purpose of the dead rising and our being caught up into the sky is not to go away but to meet Jesus as He is returning. He will not be taking us out of the world to stay. He will be lifting us up to participate with Him in His triumphal return.[113]

Sproul describes his post-tribulational view of the rapture that corresponds to a historical (covenant) premillennial position. It's not a "catching away" to Heaven; it's a calling to the air to help usher Christ to His earth.

Covenant theologians, because of an emphasis on one people of God (continuity) rather than a dispensational distinction between Israel and the Church will not teach a pre-tribulational view of the Rapture (as a general rule).

Again, generally, Covenantalists will be amillennial (thus, no rapture), pre-millennial (Jesus sets up His kingdom) or post-millennial, with a corresponding post-tribulational view of the Rapture. It would be abnormal to see a theologian with covenant leanings endorse a pre-tribulational rapture.

Remember, these differences are not insignificant. Either we are expecting the return of Jesus or we are expecting the setting up of Anti-Christ's reign for seven years. Are we looking for the Christ or the anti-Christ? Again, *it really depends on your hermeneutical presuppositions.* This chart from Moody's *Handbook of Theology* again provides a good visual understanding of these differences.

---

[113] Sproul, "What is the Rapture?" www.ligonier.org/blog/what-is-the-rapture/.

VIEWS CONCERNING LAST THINGS[114]

	Amill	Post-Mil	Historic Pre-Mil	Disp. Pre-Mil
2nd Coming	Single event; no distinction between rapture and 2nd coming	Single event; no distinction; Christ returns after Millennium	Rapture and 2nd Coming simultaneous; Christ returns to earth to reign	2nd coming in two phases: Rapture for Church; 2nd Coming 7 yrs later
Resurrection	General resurrection of believers and unbelievers	General resurrection of believers and unbelievers	Resurrection of believers at beginning of Millennium; Unbelievers at the end	Distinctions: 1 Church @ Rapture 2 OT / Trib Saints @ 2nd coming 3 Unbelievers at end of Mill.
Judgments	General for all	General for all	Judgment at 2nd coming; one at end of trib	Distinctions 1 Believer's work at Rapture 2 Jews and Gentiles at end of Trib 3 Unbelievers at end of Mill.
Tribulation	In present age	In present age	Church goes through future trib	Church raptured before future trib
Millennium	Not literal; Kingdom is present church age	Present church age blends into kingdom	Mill is both present and future, not necessarily 1000 years	Christ inaugurates 1000-year reign at His coming
Israel and Church	Church is new Israel	Church is new Israel	Some distinction. Future for Israel, but Church is spiritual Israel	Complete distinction with separate programs for each

[114] Enns, *Handbook of Theology*, 383.

Questions about Israel

When it comes to the role of modern-day Israel to prophetic fulfillment, again we find a difference between these two competing theologies. Here again, the difference is grounded in two principles: 1) What hermeneutic is utilized? and 2) Which testament receives priority (which is also related to hermeneutics)?

These differences are not based on who loves Jesus more, nor are they based on who is the godliest or most intellectual, or any other supposed characteristics for that matter. Instead, the differences, at their very core, are rooted in one's hermeneutics.

For some, the year 1948 is an important year to study and to understand its significance. It's like saying *476* (the Fall of the Roman Empire), *1492* (Columbus sailed the ocean blue), or *1776* (the establishing of an American nation) - people automatically know its importance. Likewise, 1948 will also be remembered.[115]

A big worldwide event happened: Israel was rebirthed as a nation. Did this contain prophetic overtones or did this modern-day Israeli nation have no connection to the ancient people who had inherited the land?

Behind these questions stands an even more important question: is God finished with national Israel or no? Did He divorce her for her unfaithfulness to the false gods of the land, *permanently* set her aside, and choose a new people for His name?

Or, did He set Israel aside *temporarily* so that He could fulfill His purpose through the church during this age? These are the questions that dispensationalists and covenantalists can find no common ground.

---

[115] For Californians, another major event happened in 1948: the establishment of the infamous In-N-Out Hamburger restaurants began.

Arnold Fruchtenbaum wrote a six-part article for Chafer Theological Seminary Journal in 1999. The title of his article was *Israelology*.[116] Fruchtenbaum understands the importance of his topic. In his opening, he states:

> The study of Israel is one of the major points of division in evangelical theology today. A theologian's view of Israel will determine whether he is a Covenant Theologian or a Dispensationalist.[117]

I agree with Fruchtenbaum. Two questions – when asked strategically –can reveal much about a person's theology. First, what do you think about Jesus? Secondly, what do you think about Israel? In this section, we try to tackle some of the important questions about Israel. Let's understand her origins, her current status, and her future prospects. In so doing, we'll understand that "God has not cast off Israel forever" as Paul stated in Romans 11.

The origins of the nation of Israel

In Genesis 12, an event takes place that will overshadow the rest of the Scriptures. God calls a man and enters into a covenant relationship with him. The man is Abram, later called Abraham. Genesis 12 is where the Abrahamic Covenant is introduced, with it being reiterated in chapters 15 and 17 (and alluded back to throughout the remainder of the Old Testament).

---

[116] Arnold Fruchtenbaum, "Israelology," *Chafer Theological Seminary Journal* 05:02 (April 1999). This is part one with the series spreading out over the next year.

[117] Fruchtenbaum, "Israelology," (Part 1), 28.

The contents of this covenant include a land, a promised seed, and a special blessing for each family of the earth. The land aspect - a specific land promised to a specific people - would be enhanced through the Land Covenant (sometimes called the Palestinian Covenant). The seed aspect would be enlarged through the Davidic Covenant. The blessing aspect would be greatly focused through the New Covenant.

Even more important than the contents of this covenant would be the type of covenant it is. Theologians have described this specific covenant with words like *eternal*, *unconditional*, and *literal*. Nowhere does the promises contained in the Abrahamic Covenant get cancelled or transferred. This truth led Paul to say that God would not cast off Israel forever (Romans 11.1). God has a future plan for Israel because He is bound by an oath, a covenant.

When we say the Abrahamic Covenant is unconditional, this is an important point to consider. When God comes to ratify this covenant with Abraham in Genesis 15, we find Abraham cutting animals in half. It's a strange scene! In the biblical world, they didn't "make" covenants – they literally "cut a covenant."

In a covenant between two equal parties, the conditions would be understood prior to the making of the official covenant. Once the parties were ready to "cut the covenant," they would both walk through the midst of sacrificed animals. This symbolically stated something to the effect of, "If I don't honor my part of the covenant, may this happen to me…"

What's important in Genesis 15 is that God caused a deep sleep to come upon Abraham so that *only* God walked through the midst. This is the basis for calling this *unconditional*.

As stated previously, dispensationalists hold to a normal hermeneutic.[118] When we read that God would give Abraham's descendants a specific land, and that from his seed would come the Promised One who would be a blessing for all families – we must take that at face value.

God's choice of Abraham out of all the earth was not the end of His choices. Abraham had two sons, Ishmael and Isaac. God chose Isaac. Isaac had two sons, Esau and Jacob. God chose Jacob. Jacob had twelve sons - God chose Judah. Eventually, he would choose Boaz, Jesse, and David. He was preparing a nation and also providing a means through which to fulfill the promises embedded in Genesis 3.15.

Abraham's descendants spent some time in Egypt - 430 years! But God eventually sent a deliverer, Moses. God led Moses and Israel to Mount Sinai where God would enter into another covenant with Israel - the Mosaic Covenant, or Law. This serves as the founding (officially) of a nation, devoted to their God, and prepared to claim the land that Jehovah had granted them.

Throughout the Old Testament, God used judges, kings, and prophets to direct His people in the way they should go. They enjoyed good kings such as David and Solomon and endured wicked kings like Jeconiah. Yet, God continued working on their behalf. In wrath, He remembered mercy.

---

[118] Any word used to describe one's hermeneutic is a loaded term. Here, I use the word *normal* – yet, I realize that this implies that any other method is not normal. At other times, I have referred to this as the *common-sense* approach. Yet, again, that can imply that those who use a different approach just don't have "common sense." I'm not trying to be offensive with these terms. The technical terms *historical-grammatical* sometimes needs a "face" to help people understand. These descriptors state that a dispensational hermeneutic takes the text at face value.

153

The current status the nation of Israel

God made several covenants with this people group after the Abrahamic Covenant. For most of the Old Testament narrative, the children of Israel lived under the Mosaic Covenant. During this time, the Land Covenant was reiterated. Some refer to this as the Palestinian Covenant - but the name is purposely offensive. The word *Palestinian* is a derivative of the ancient enemy of Israel, the *Philistines*.

This is observed by Richard Nyrop. He writes, "After the 132-135 revolt, the Roman emperor Hadrian renamed the area Syria Palestina."[119] Subsequently, he then began to disperse the Jews. He converted their temple into a place to worship Jupiter.

Hadrian renamed the land of Israel "Palestine" to punish the Jewish people for their rebellion. Jerusalem was now renamed Aelia Capitolina, and Jews were forbidden to enter the city. The province was named Syria-Palestina (→ Palestine), after Israel's former enemies, the Philistines.[120] It was the proverbial "slap-in-the-face" from the conqueror showing whose boss.

Later in the Old Testament, God provided His people with the Davidic and the New covenants. There were some setbacks, to be sure. The Assyrian and Babylonian captivities were such times. Yet, as one considered the promises embedded in the covenants - the future looked bright.

Through all of the wars with the Philistine, Syrian, Hellenistic, and Roman kingdoms —always the belief that Messiah was coming

---

[119] Richard Nyrop, *Area Handbook for the Hashemite Kingdom of Jordan* (Washington, DC: American University, 1974), 10.

[120] Antonius Gunneweg, Marianne Awerbuch, & Charles Kimball, "Israel," *The Encyclopedia of Christianity* (Grand Rapids: Eerdmans; 1999), 773.

remained in the forefront of their minds. But when He came, He wasn't the political ruler they were expecting…*so they put their own king to death*. To put it mildly, everything changed for the nation after this.

What do you do when your temple is destroyed, your animal sacrifices are stopped, you lose your land, and you're scattered throughout the world? This was the situation that Israel found herself in. In the book of Romans, Paul describes Israel's past (chapter 9), her present (chapter 10), and her future (chapter 11). Spiritually, he described Israel as being in a state of blindness.

Generally speaking, Jewish people are not easy to evangelize. They reject the claims of Jesus as their Messiah. They reject the authenticity of the New Testament. They find the term "Old Testament" offensive. Currently, they are in blindness and God's plan for Israel is not moving forward.

In 1948, a nation was born in a day. Occupying land about the size of New Jersey, modern-day Israel was declared by the United Nations as an independent state. Dispensationalists saw prophetic fulfillment as Jewish people were coming back to the land. Covenant theologians saw no prophetic fulfillment, noting that "we can't be really sure if these are actually descendants of the biblical Jews."

Currently, Israel is in her land.[121] She is spiritually blinded and gospel-hardened. The promises and plans God had stated for Israel are not being pursued at this moment. The question everyone debates: Is God finished with national Israel or not? Has the church become the spiritual fulfillment for the promises made to Israel? Is the church the replacement for Israel? Has she superseded Israel? Or, does God have a future plan that involves Israel?

---

[121] At least, partially. It will not be until the kingdom age when Israel finally regains all the territory promised to her.

155

Understand, no one denies that God is not interceding for the world through national Israel *at this time.* That's not the question or the debate. Rather, the question is, "Will God minister to the world through national Israel *in the future?*

The future prospects for the nation of Israel

These questions show the importance of one's hermeneutics. The question concerning the future of Israel is largely answered for believers based upon the way they read the Bible. In Romans 11, dispensationalists believe that Paul makes the case that God is not finished with national Israel.

If Israel means *physical* descendants of Abraham, Isaac, and Jacob - and if it is distinct from the church made up of Jews and Gentiles - then a normal reading of the Old Testament would cause believers to anticipate at least the following:

1. Israel will be permanently restored to the full boundaries of the land God gave to her (Ezekiel 37).
2. Israel will evangelize the world during the tribulation (144,000 Jewish Witnesses).
3. Israel will accept her Messiah (Zech 12.10).
4. Israel will enjoy a literal messianic kingdom (the Millennium).
5. Israel will be protected from her enemies during the tribulation (Daniel 11.41; Rev 12).
6. All nations will come to Jerusalem to see the King (Micah 4:1-2).
7. A Jewish temple will be rebuilt (Ezekiel 40-48).
8. Sacrifices will be once again offered during the kingdom (Ezekiel 43-46).

Dispensationalists read the Bible and take all of it in its plain sense. The Abrahamic Covenant, mentioned in Genesis 12, is expounded upon in Genesis 15 and 17. Consider Genesis 17.7-8 for just one moment. Jehovah says that He will establish the covenant with Abraham and with His seed as an *everlasting* covenant.

Then, in reference to the land, He specifically states that He will give it to Abraham's seed as an *everlasting* possession. In Romans 11, as Paul discusses the future for Israel, he tells us that the gifts and callings of God are without repentance – that is, they are irrevocable. God gave an *everlasting* covenant that included an *everlasting* possession that is rooted in God's *everlasting* faithfulness and thus, *irrevocable*.

A theological conundrum?

How do other theological systems get around these truths? Usually, one of three solutions are presented: 1) God's promises would be fulfilled with *spiritual* Israel, rather than physical Israel, 2) Jesus is the New Israel and all prophecies are fulfilled in Him, or 3) Israel has forfeited her inheritance and God has given it to another. Generally, this utilizes language such as, "God has divorced Israel."

To be clear, those people who believe Scripture contains no future promises for Israel still have a love for God's Word. They are sincere Christians who have a heart for God, for holiness, and are living waiting for Jesus to return. Their understanding of no future for Israel is simply the result of their hermeneutics.

Bruce Waltke is representative of the "no promised future for Israel" view. He was a contributor to the book *Continuity and Discontinuity*, writing a chapter entitled "Kingdom Promises as Spiritual." The warnings to Israel were to be taken *literal*. The blessings to Israel were to be understood as *spiritual*. He states, "It

157

will be concluded that the kingdom promises are comprehensively fulfilled in the church, not in restored national Israel.[122]"

Consider the words of theologian Herman Ridderbos. His view of the future of Israel left nothing to be questioned.

> The church as the people of the New Covenant has taken the place of Israel, and national Israel is nothing other than the empty shell from which the pearl has been removed and which has lost its function in the history of redemption.[123]

Other theologians take a different approach. Rather than say the church replaces Israel, they teach that all of national Israel's prophecies have been fulfilled in Christ. Here are a few samplings to help you understand their view:

> For Paul, Christ had gathered up the promise into the singularity of his own person…The land, like the Law, particular and provisional, had become irrelevant.[124]

> Horton similarly describes national Israel and its calling as "typological of the true Israel, the faithful Adam, who is the true heavenly temple and everlasting Sabbath of God."[125]

---

[122] Bruce K. Waltke, "Kingdom Promises as Spiritual," in *Continuity and Discontinuity: Perspectives on the Relationship between the Old and New Testaments.* ed. John S. Feinberg (Westchester: Crossway, 1988), 262–263.

[123] Herman Ridderbos, *Paul: An Outline of His Theology* (Grand Rapids: Eerdmans, 1975), 354-355.

[124] W.D. Davies, *The Gospel and the Land* (Berkeley, CA: University of California, 1974), 179.

[125] Robert Saucy, "Is Christ the Fulfillment of National Israel's Prophecies? Yes and No!" *The Master's Seminary Journal* (Spring 2017): 17-29.

No dispensationalist would argue that Jesus didn't fulfill prophecies or that He was the perfect Jew. Yet, agreeing with this doesn't mean that there is no place for national Israel in the future. If the hermeneutic we have argued for is the correct approach – and if the Old Testament is the starting point for reading the Scriptures – then these two pillars of hermeneutics dogmatically point to the conclusion that God has a future plan for Israel.

For a sampling of those who hold that Israel has been divorced by God, Brewer's opening remarks from his article should suffice:

> God is described in the Old Testament as married
> to Israel and Judah, and in the New Testament the church is
> described as the Bride of Christ. The marriage
> to Israel ended in divorce and the marriage to Judah suffered
> a period of separation. Paul suggests that this marriage
> ended when Christ died, in order that Christ would be free
> to marry the Church with a better marriage covenant.[126]

According to Brewer's view, God *permanently* divorced Israel, meaning the ten northern tribes whose capital was Samaria. He *temporarily* separated from Judah, the southern two tribes, during the Babylonian Captivity. He attempted to reconcile, but His death allowed Him to be free from that marriage. He took the out – the loophole provided by the law – and married the church. Together, they enjoyed the New Covenant and were happy ever after.

In Jeremiah 31.31, God promises to the Jewish nation that He would bring about a "new covenant." It's described in verses 31-34. Here's the passage so we can see it together:

---

[126] David Brewer, "Three Weddings and a Divorce: God's Covenant with Israel, Judah, and the Church." *Tyndale Bulletin* 47:1 (1996): 1-26.

Behold, the days come, saith the LORD, that I will make a new covenant with the house of Israel, and with the house of Judah: Not according to the covenant that I made with their fathers in the day that I took them by the hand to bring them out of the land of Egypt; which my covenant they brake, although I was an husband unto them, saith the LORD: But this shall be the covenant that I will make with the house of Israel; After those days, saith the LORD, I will put my law in their inward parts, and write it in their hearts; and will be their God, and they shall be my people. And they shall teach no more every man his neighbor, and every man his brother, saying, Know the LORD: for they shall all know me, from the least of them unto the greatest of them, saith the LORD: for I will forgive their iniquity, and I will remember their sin no more.

Read those verses carefully. Imagine that you are living in Jeremiah's day. Babylon is amassing its forces. They have already carried some of your friends away. Daniel and Ezekiel are now removed from the land. You know the judgment of God is coming soon. As you consider Jeremiah's words in this context, notice these basic truths about the new covenant:

1. It is with the house of Israel and Judah
2. It's different from the Mosaic Covenant
3. God was a husband to the Jewish nation
4. His new covenant will be inward, not on tables of stone
5. The knowledge of the Lord will fill the earth
6. The sins of the Jewish people will be forever forgiven

For those who say God has divorced His wife forever, they miss the context. Israel is already gone at the time of this prophecy. She was carried away by Assyria. Judah is at the zero hour for the

Babylonian Captivity. Yet, in the midst of all this judgement, God is promising both houses a *future* with Him.

If this wasn't a clear indication of His intent, we only need to keep reading the next few verses. Consider what God says in verses 35-37 (Jeremiah 31).

> Thus saith the LORD, which giveth the sun for a light by day, and the ordinances of the moon and of the stars for a light by night, which divideth the sea when the waves thereof roar; The LORD of hosts is his name: If those ordinances depart from before me, saith the LORD, then the seed of Israel also shall cease from being a nation before me for ever. Thus saith the LORD; If heaven above can be measured, and the foundations of the earth searched out beneath, I will also cast off all the seed of Israel for all that they have done, saith the LORD.

If the sun, moon, and stars stop giving their light, then Israel will cease being a nation. If man can ever measure Heaven and search out the foundations of the earth, then He will cast off all the seed of Israel. This is pure rhetoric on the Lord's behalf. He is saying, "I know what Israel has done...I also know that I am bound to them with an eternal covenant...I will never forget the sure mercies I gave to David...Israel has a future with Me!"

There is only one view that teaches God's *everlasting* covenant and Israel's *everlasting* possession of the land applies to national Israel. That one view is the one espoused by a normal reading of the text. God promised the land to Abraham, to Isaac, to Jacob - to the physical descendants of Abraham. Dispensationalism alone, based upon the hermeneutics already discussed, believes the only way God's promises can be fulfilled is if there is a future for Israel.

Summary

As you have gathered from the last two chapters, the dispensationalist tries to consistently use the normal, literal, historical-grammatical approach - even in the prophetic Scriptures. This commitment does cause some disagreements with Christians who are *usually* literal in their approach, but not always.

We can't answer, "Does the Church go through the Tribulation?" without dealing with hermeneutical issues. If we are to interpret the promises to Israel literally, then the answer is "No." If we are to interpret the promises *spiritually*, the answer moves to either "Yes" or "Maybe."

But notice that as soon as we interpret promises to Israel *spiritually*, then our "Israelology" is affected. There is no *biblical* reason to befriend the nation of Israel because God is finished with Israel (if we take this approach).

You may be starting to think, "I thought this was an introduction to dispensationalism, but I'm starting to think it's more of a hermeneutical book!" If so, that's intentional. Dispensationalism isn't an acknowledgement of the three non-negotiables. Rather, it's an understanding of a *hermeneutical* system that helps us understand God's revelation to man.

Chapter 7

CONCLUSION

All good things must come to an end!

"There is no real ending. It's just the place where you stop the story."
Frank Herbert

It's time to bring this part of our conversation to an end. As we wrap things up, I wanted to provide a quick review and leave some parting comments. Just in case you've not figured it out yet, I believe this topic is vitally important to the way we understand our Bibles.

Three Non-Negotiables

Dispensationalism isn't just a system - it's a *hermeneutical* system. This hermeneutic is characterized by its adherence to three simple rules. These three are the non-negotiables and form the backbone for this system.

1. Our model for understanding the text is rooted in a *consistent* use of the normal, historical-grammatical interpretative process. Because of an emphasis on *historical* aspects, the New Testament is not read back into the Old Testament nor does it change the single meaning of that text.

2. Because of our interpretative approach, we see a difference between Israel and the church. In eternity, we will all enjoy God's kingdom together. In "time," God has managed His house differently.

3. Our unifying purpose to understanding God's revelation is a doxological one. The principle of God's glory is what ties everything together.

Darby is not the Final Authority

While not minimizing Darby's influence on dispensationalism, we have stressed two points. First, the seeds for dispensationalism are rooted in the early church fathers. Secondly, American dispensationalism looks differently from what Darby taught.

We have looked at the primary and secondary characteristics within each dispensation. We've noticed that some things are brought over from one dispensation to the next while others are not. The Bible is our guide in what carries over. Those things that carry over and are still binding for New Testament believers constitute the Law of Christ.

There is a Difference

As we have compared and contrasted dispensationalism and covenant theology, we have observed that there really are differences. These differences – be they differences about the church, about end times, about salvation, or about Israel – stem from two foundational principles. First, covenant theology is not always consistently literal in its interpretation of prophecies. Secondly, the New Testament is given priority as the starting point for hermeneutics within Covenant Theology.

These presuppositional biases (and again, I have these as well) cause scholars from each side to read the same text and come to two different conclusions.

Theological disagreements do not need to create theological enemies. Yet, integrity causes us to note that the impasse is a fairly large one to cross. Today, segments from both sides are attempting to build bridges. Progressive Dispensationalists blur the distinction between Church and Israel. Their complementary interpretation at times leads to the same conclusions as a covenantalist.

On the other side, New Covenant Theology seeks to find the strengths of dispensationalism and covenant theology as a synthesis. Both progressive dispensationalism and new covenant theology reside in the middle ground between the two systems contrasted in this book. The desire to find common ground is noble; the cost of losing one's distinctiveness, however, is high.

A dispensationalist can appreciate the high view of Scripture, a belief that God is control, and its strong emphasis on biblical preaching espoused in Reformed Theology. Hopefully the covenantalist can appreciate the dispensationalist's desire to interpret Scripture as it would have been understood by its original audience and its contribution to biblical, exegetical preaching as well.

A sincere expression of gratitude

As we come to the end, I hope this book has answered some questions. Yet, I hope it has raised a few as well. Questions indicate that thinking is taking place...and that's a good thing! This will not be the last book written on this important subject, but hopefully it will provide a starting point for many to consider the merits of dispensationalism.

At the end of the day, whether you accept the premise of the book or reject it, hopefully we can all agree that the Bible deserves our most diligent efforts in attempting to understand it.

Thanks for taking this journey with me!

Appendix

The Hermeneutical Circle

Background | Introduction

Exegesis

MEANING

Presuppositions

Biblical Theology

Historical Theology

SIGNIFICANCE

Practical Theology

Systematic Theology

Literally, an entire class could be taught on how to use this circle. Let me provide a few instructions and hopefully give you a tool that you can use in your own study of biblical texts.

Orientation

The circle runs clockwise, starting with Presuppositions. It travels through the introductory, exegetical and biblical theological stages. Step five (Historical Theology) is what bridges the cultural and historical divide between the MEANING and the SIGNIFICANCE (application) of the text.

Once the text is understood in its own context, step six branches out to a more systematic approach, followed by how to make it all practical for today's believer. The arrow at the end reminds us that as a result of going through this process, the next time we come to the same text, our presuppositions may be different, and we should be able to go even deeper into the text.

Steps in the Process

As much as we want to be, it's virtually impossible to be purely objective with a text. The reason for this is because we are all affected by the books we've read, the sermons we've heard (maybe the ones we've preached) and all of the other social media and influencers in our lives. All of this affects our thinking and we start to "presuppose" things without demanding proof. It's our assumptions - and they are not all bad.

Step one challenges the interpreter to list out his presuppositions. Here are a few of mine that I always have:

1. The Bible is the Word of God
2. Jesus is God
3. The Pauline Epistles were written by Paul

4. The New Testament was finished before the end of the first century.

I don't prove these points every time I open my Bible…I assume them to be true. However, there are times when going through this process causes a conflict between my presupposed truths and what the text actually teaches. At that moment, I have an integrity crisis…I need to stay humble before the text.

Step two involves the historical aspect in the *historical-grammatical* interpretation. I'm now asking my journalist questions. Who wrote this? To whom did he write? Why did he write? Where was he when he wrote? Where were they? What's going on in the world during this time? Was there an event that provided the opportunity for writing? Are there problems being dealt with?

In other words, I want to know everything I can know about this book. Then, when I am teaching through it, these lessons I learn help me to paint a picture for the audience. My goal as a communicator is to make the text visible to my hearers. Can I describe a location? Can I provide a picture for a visual aid?

Step three is actually delving into the text. *Exegesis* is a fancy word that simply means we are pulling the meaning "out of" (ex-) the text. At this point, we are defining words. We are looking for commands. Meaning can only be understood clearly if a context is given.

Here is my favorite example to use about the importance of context. I want to share with you a complete sentence, with only four words. Every word is a one-syllable word. You will not need a dictionary to recognize these simple, every-day words. Yet, *you will not understand the meaning of the sentence!*

That was a ball.

No dictionary needed. Yet, without a context, you don't know what it means. Is it colloquial: "I had a great time!" Is it formal and indicative of an elegant ballroom you've just attended? Is it an innocent child answering, "What's that?" Are we at a sporting event with the umpire saying, "That was strike...That was a ball..."? We just don't know!

So, in step three, it is inadequate to simply define some words and say, "Well, the *Greek* means..." More important is to note that, "According to the context, the *writer* means..."

In **step four,** we move to something called *biblical theology*. This is an attempt to understand one of two elements: 1) What was the understanding on that subject up to that point in progressive revelation, or 2) How did that particular writer explain that subject elsewhere? We aren't running through the entire Bible. We are looking at a cross section.

It may be easier to illustrate than to define biblical theology. Imagine that you are preaching a sermon on *love* and want to understand the New Testament passage thoroughly. At this step, you may ask, "How was the concept of *love* understood in the first century?" Additionally, you may also ask, "What did Paul [or Peter, John, etc] teach about this elsewhere? This process is the biblical theological approach.

In **step five,** we ask, "How has the church handled this passage [this topic] for the last 2,000 years. It's a checks and balances system to ensure that we don't teach the proverbial, "No one has ever seen this in the Bible before me!" There's usually a reason for that!

In **step six,** we broaden from just the local time frame to trace the subject systematically throughout the Bible. Systematic theology is really just an accumulation of various biblical theologies put together to show the entire picture.

The **final step** really answers the question, "So what?" What do we do with this knowledge, this command, this promise? How do we live today differently because of this truth? This is the application stage that bridges the cultural and historical divide from the biblical world to our world today.

Then, you'll notice that after going through this process, it should affect your presuppositions. So, the next time you go through this passage, you're starting from a slightly different understanding and able to dig a little deeper into the text.

Summary

A workman needeth not to be ashamed... Interpreting the Bible requires some work! This process described in this short overview is only a tool - but I've found it be a helpful tool as I work through different passages.

Warning: It may be awkward and difficult at first, but if you stick with it, the rewards are pretty encouraging!

Bibliography

Adams, Jay. *Competent to Counsel: Introduction to Nouthetic Counseling*. Grand Rapids: Ministry Resources Library, 1986.

Alexis, Jonas. *Christianity and Rabbinic Judaism: A History of Conflict Vol 2*. Bloomington, IN: Westbow Press, 2013.

Bateman, Herbert. *Three Central Issues in Contemporary Dispensationalism*. Grand Rapids: Kregel, 1999.

Bass, Clarence. *Backgrounds to Dispensationalism*. Grand Rapids: Eerdmans, 1960.

Berkhof, L. *Systematic Theology*. Grand Rapids: Eerdmans, 1938.

Bigalke, Ron J. *Progressive Dispensationalism: An Analysis of the Movement and Defense of Traditional Dispensationalism*. Lanham, MD: University Press of America, 2005.

Boice, James. *Foundations of the Christian Faith: A Comprehensive and Readable Theology*. Downers Grove: InterVarsity, 2019.

Bray, John. *The Origin of the Pre-Tribulation Rapture Teaching*. Lakeland, FL: self-published, 1982.

Brentnall, J.M. "Two Dispensations: One Salvation." Banner Truth. https://banneroftruth.org/us/resources/articles/2012/two-dispensations-one-salvation/.

Brewer, David. "Three Weddings and a Divorce: God's Covenant with Israel, Judah, and the Church." *Tyndale Bulletin* 47:1 (1996): 1-26.

Calvin, John. *Institutes of the Christian Religion*. London: Wolfe and Harison, 1561.

Chafer, Lewis Sperry. *Dispensationalism*. Dallas, TX: Dallas Theological Seminary, 1936.

-----. "Inventing Heretics Through Misunderstanding." *Bibliotheca Sacra* 102 (Jan 1945): 1.

Chumney, Eddie. *The Seven Festivals of Messiah*. Http:/hebroots.com/sevenfestivals.

Cone, Christopher. *Prolegomena on Biblical Hermeneutics and Method*, 2nd Edition. Hurst, TX: Tyndale Seminary, 2012.

Cooper, Lamar Eugene. *Ezekiel*. Vol. 17, The New American Commentary. Nashville: Broadman & Holman Publishers, 1994.

Corley, Bruce; Steve Lemke, and Grant Lovejoy. *Biblical Hermeneutics: A Comprehensive Introduction to Interpreting Scripture*, 2nd ed. Nashville, TN: Broadman & Holman, 2002.

Darby, John Nelson. *On 'Days' Signifying 'Years' in Prophetic Language*. 1830. CW2:35.

-----. *Studies on the Book of Daniel*. 1848. CW5:151.

Davies, W.D. *The Gospel and the Land*. Berkeley, CA: University of California, 1974.

Enns, Paul P., *The Moody Handbook of Theology*. Chicago, IL: Moody Press, 1989.

Erickson, Millard. *Christian Theology*. Grand Rapids: Baker, 1998.

Eusebius. Ecclesiastical History, iii.39.12.

Feinberg, John. Editor, *Continuity and Discontinuity: Perspectives on the Relationship Between the Old and New Testaments*. Westchester, IL: Crossway Books, 1988.

Finney, Jerald. *God Betrayed: Separation of Church and State: The Biblical Principles and the American Application*. Austin, TX: Kerygma Publishing, 2008.

Freeley, Austin J. and David L. Steinberg. *Argumentation and Debate: Critical Thinking for Reasoned Decision Making*. Wadsworth CENGAGE Learning, 2009.

Fruchtenbaum, Arnold. "Israelology." *Chafer Theological Seminary Journal* 05:02 (April 1999).

Galli, Mark and Ted Olsen. "Introduction," in *131 Christians Everyone Should Know*. Nashville: B & H, 2000.

Gregg, Steve. "Is Dispensationalism Indispensable," Feb 7, 2015. **https://www.equip.org/article/dispensationalism-indispensable/**.

Grudem, Wayne. *Systematic Theology: An Introduction to Biblical Doctrine*. Grand Rapids: Zondervan, 2004.

Gunneweg, Antonius H. J.; Marianne Awerbuch, and Charles A. Kimball. "Israel," *The Encyclopedia of Christianity*. Grand Rapids: Wm. B. Eerdmans; Brill, 1999–2003.

Harbach, Robert. "Dispensationalism: An Ancient Error." First published in 1967. Protestant Reformed Churches in America. http://www.prca.org/resources/publications/articles/item/3741-dispensationalism-an-ancient-error.

Hirsch, E.D. *Validity in Interpretation*. Yale University, 1967.

Hixson, J. B. and Mark Fontecchio. *What Lies Ahead: A Biblical Overview of the End Times*. Brenham, TX: Lucid Books, 2013.

Hodge, Charles. *Systematic Theology*. Grand Rapids: Eerdmans, 1981.

Ice, Thomas. "A Short History of Dispensationalism." *Article Archives* (2009): 37.

-----. "The Rapture in Pseudo-Ephraem." https://pre-trib.org/pretribfiles/pdfs/Ice-TheRaptureinPseudo-Ephraem.pdf.

Irenaeus of Lyons. "Irenæus against Heresies," in *The Apostolic Fathers with Justin Martyr and Irenaeus*. Ed. Alexander Roberts, Donaldson, and Coxe, vol. 1, The Ante-Nicene Fathers. Buffalo, NY: Christian Literature Company, 1885.

Jeremiah, David. "Living with Confidence in a Chaotic World," sermon at https://www.youtube.com/watch?v=-jz4DEljlVw.

MacPherson, David. *The Great Rapture Hoax*. Fletcher, NC: New Puritan Library, 1983.

Martyr, Justin. "Dialogue of Justin with Trypho, a Jew," in *The Apostolic Fathers with Justin Martyr and Irenaeus*. Ed. Alexander Roberts, James Donaldson, and A. Cleveland Coxe, vol. 1, The Ante-Nicene Fathers. Buffalo, NY: Christian Literature Company, 1885.

-----. "The First Apology of Justin," in *The Apostolic Fathers with Justin Martyr and Irenaeus*. Ed. Alexander Roberts, James Donaldson, and A. Cleveland Coxe, vol. 1, The Ante-Nicene Fathers. Buffalo, NY: Christian Literature Company, 1885.

McCune, Rolland. *A Systematic Theology of Biblical Christianity: Prolegomena and the Doctrines of Scripture, God, and Angels*. Vol. 1. Allen Park, MI: Detroit Baptist Theological, 2009.

-----. *A Systematic Theology of Biblical Christianity*. Vol. 3. Detroit: Detroit Baptist Theological, 2010.

Merkley, Benjamin. *Discontinuity to Continuity: A Survey of Dispensational and Covenantal Theologies*. Bellingham, WA: Lexham Press, 2020.

Merritt, Jonathan. "Understanding the Evangelical Obsession with Israel." *America: The Jesuit Review* (December, 2017).

Metcalfe, John. *Deliverance from the Law: The Westminster Confession Exploded*. John Metcalfe Publishing Trust, 1992.

Murray, David. "Our View of the Old Testament." *Puritan Reformed Journal* 02:2 (July 2010): 5.

Nyrop, Richard. *Area Handbook for the Hashemite Kingdom of Jordan*. Washington, DC: American University, 1974.

Oyer, John. "Sticks and Stones Broke Their Bones, and Vicious Names Did Hurt Them!" *Christian History Magazine-Issue 5: Radical Reformation: The Anabaptists* (Worcester, PA: Christian History Institute, 1985).

Payne, J. Barton. *An Outline of Hebrew History*. Grand Rapids: Baker, 1954.

Pentecost, J. Dwight. "Daniel," in *The Bible Knowledge Commentary: An Exposition of the Scriptures*. Ed. John F. Walvoord and Roy B. Zuck. Vol. 1. Wheaton, IL: Victor Books, 1985.

-----. *Things to Come: A Study in Biblical Eschatology*. Grand Rapids: Zondervan, 1958.

Pickering, Ernest. "Dispensational Theology." *Central Bible Quarterly* 04:1 (Spring 1961): 29-35.

-----. "The Nature of Covenant Theology." *Central Bible Quarterly* 3, No. 4 (Winter 1960): 1-8.

Poythress, Vern. *Understanding Dispensationalists*. Grand Rapids: Zondervan, 1987.

Ramm, Bernard. *Protestant Biblical Interpretation: A Textbook of Hermeneutics*, Third Revised Edition. Grand Rapids, MI: Baker Books, 1970.

Reardon, Parker. "Dispensationalism 101 – Part 3." http://dispensationalpublishing.com/issues-of-contention-part-1-ecclesiology-and-eschatology/.

Reeves, Chris. "The People of God: A Study of the Continuity and Discontinuity Between OT Israel and the NT Church." https://thegoodteacher.com/Special/The%20People%20of%20God%20(Reeves).pdf.

Ridderbos, Herman. *Paul: An Outline of His Theology*. Grand Rapids: Eerdmans, 1975.

Ryrie, Charles. *Basic Theology: A Popular Systematic Guide to Understanding Biblical Truth*. Chicago: Moody, 1986.

-----. *Dispensationalism*. Chicago: Moody, 1995.

-----. "The End of the Law." *Bibliotheca Sacra* 124 (July-September, 1967): 246.

Saucy, Robert. "Is Christ the Fulfillment of National Israel's Prophecies? Yes and No!" *The Master's Seminary Journal* (Spring 2017): 17-29.

Schmidtbleicher, Paul. "Law in the New Testament." *Chafer Theological Journal* 09:02 (Fall 2003): 50-79.

Scofield, C. I. *Rightly Dividing the Word of Truth (2 Tim. 2:15): Ten Outline Studies of the More Important Divisions of Scripture*. Philadelphia: Philadelphia School of the Bible, 1921.

Scroggie, Graham. *The Unfolding Drama of Redemption*. Grand Rapids: Kregel Classics, 1995.

Showers, Renald, "An Introduction to Dispensational Theology." http://gracebiblestudies.org/resources/Web.

-----. *There Really is a Difference*. Bellmawr, NJ: Friends of Israel Ministry, 1990.

Slick, Matt. "What is Dispensationalism?" CARM, https://carm.org/dispensationalism.

Sproul, R.C. "The Covenant of Works." https://www.monergism.com/thethreshold/articles/onsite/covenantworks.html.

-----. "What is the Rapture?" https://www.ligonier.org/blog/what-is-the-rapture/.

Spurgeon, Charles. *Spurgeon's Sermons*. Volume 15: 1869. London.

Stallard, Mike. Editor, *Dispensational Understanding of the New Covenant*. Schaumburg, IL: Regular Baptist Press, 2012.

Thiessen, Henry Clarence and Vernon D. Doerksen. *Lectures in Systematic Theology*. Grand Rapids: Eerdmans, 1979.

Toussiant, Stanley. *Acts*. In the Bible Knowledge Commentary. Wheaton, IL: Victor, 1983.

Utley, Robert James. *You Can Understand the Bible!* Marshall, TX: Bible Lessons International, 1996.

Vlach, Michael. *Dispensationalism: Essential Beliefs and Common Myths*. Los Angeles: Theological Studies Press, 2008.

-----. http://mikevlach.blogspot.com/2016/12/dispensationalism-and-continuity.html.

Waltke, Bruce K. "Kingdom Promises as Spiritual," in *Continuity and Discontinuity: Perspectives on the Relationship between the Old and New Testaments: Essays in Honor of S. Lewis Johnson, Jr.*, ed. John Feinberg (Westchester, IL: Crossway, 1988.

Walvoord, John F. "Why I Believe the Bible." https://walvoord.com/article/316.

White, Randy, "The Dispensational Principle of Carryover, Part 2" https://dispensationalpublishing.com/the-dispensational-principle-of-carryover-part-2/.

Yarchin, William. *History of Biblical Interpretation*. Grand Rapids: Baker Academic, 2004.

Zodhiates, Spiros. *The Complete Word Study Dictionary: New Testament*. Chattanooga, TN: AMG Publishers, 2000.

Additional books by J. Michael Lester

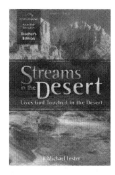

Streams in the Desert is a 13-week adult or teen Sunday school curriculum. The lessons are based on life principles and applications from thirteen individuals who witnessed God's transforming power in the desert.

This book is available through http://strivingtogether.com.

Rightly Divided is a true beginner's guide to bible study. The book introduces practical tips for correctly understanding God's Word and provides opportunities to put those principles into practice.

Available at http://strivingtogether.com or at http://amazon.com for Kindle edition.

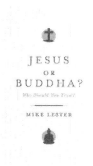

Estimates state that there are 535 million Buddhists in our world today. No doubt, much sincerity is held by these proponents.

In *Jesus or Buddha?*, readers are invited to compare and contrast the claims made by both Jesus and the Buddha. In the end, who should we trust.

Available at http://strivingtogether.com

About the author

I grew up in a pastor's home in the state of Georgia. The Bible has always been a part of my life. My granddad was a pastor – great-granddad as well. Many of my uncles have been in ministry also.

I went to Bible college in Tennessee and met the woman God had for me! We were married in 1995, and shortly after we moved to California to serve at Lancaster Baptist Church and West Coast Baptist College. We have five daughters, two sons-in-laws, one granddaughter, and Bexley, our faithful yorkie-poo!

In ministry, I serve as the academic dean of West Coast Baptist College and enjoy teaching Bible classes both on-campus and online. I serve as one of the singles' pastors at our church.

Regardless of the venue, my desire is to see people not only read the Bible, but also understand it. Sometimes I say it this way: "Learn the Book; Love the Book; and Live the Book!"

I hope this book has helped me accomplish that goal in your life. I sincerely trust that your desire to study God's Word has been fueled in a greater way as a result of our time together. If you've been helped, consider checking out my blog at jmichaellester.com where I blog with the goal of helping believers be equipped to know God's Word and to rightly divide it!